The Lure of Divine Love

The Lure of Divine Love

*Human Experience and Christian
Faith in a Process Perspective*

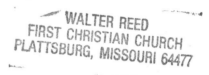

Norman Pittenger

The Pilgrim Press • New York City
T. & T. Clark Limited • Edinburgh

Library of Congress Cataloging in Publication Data

Pittenger, William Norman, 1905–
   The lure of divine love.

   1. Process theology—Addresses, essays, lectures.
I. Title.
BT83.6.P57   230   79-15611
ISBN 0-8298-0370-X

The Pilgrim Press, 287 Park Avenue South, New York, New York 10010

T. & T. Clark Limited,
36 George Street,
Edinburgh EH2 2LQ, Scotland

Contents

Preface

The material in this book had its origin in lectures delivered in the United Kingdom, the United States, and Canada. Part One, here called "Human Experience and Process Thought," was given on the Alexander Brown Foundation as a series of lectures at Randolph-Macon College, Ashland, Virginia, U.S.A. in 1976; the material in Part Two, here called "God in Process: Christian Faith and Process Thought," was a series of lectures given at St. Augustine's College, Canterbury, England in 1966.

Part One appears in print for the first time. Some of it I used in lectures at places other than Randolph-Macon, and I used it in its entirety at a clergy conference in Utah in the States and before students at the College of Emmanuel and St. Chad in Saskatoon, Saskatchewan, Canada. Part Two was published in 1967 under the title *God in Process* by the Student Christian Movement Press, London, as one of their SCM Paperbacks. Within about three years, the entire stock was sold and the book went out of print. Since then I have received hundreds of requests that it once again be made available; but a new edition did not seem feasible.

Last year, I was approached by T. and T. Clark of Edinburgh with the suggestion that SCM Press might return to me the rights on that book and a new, and updated, edition might be published. I agreed to this and SCM Press consented. But in my discussions with Dr. Geoffrey Green of Clark's, I told him that The Pilgrim Press in New York was to publish the Alexander Brown lectures and I asked about the possibility of combining the two in a single volume. To my delight, Clark's accepted this idea, and Pilgrim Press gave their hearty approval. Thus the book now in the reader's hands is a revised version of the two originals. They are arranged so that they complement each other in their discussion of what is now called *The Lure of Divine Love: Human Experience and Christian Faith in a Process Perspective.*

Were I to dedicate this book to anyone, it would be to the students and faculty of Randolph-Macon College and the College of Emmanuel and St. Chad. In particular, I should wish it to be "for" several students at the latter institution, who during my three months as a visiting professor there showed me such loving friendship: David Asher, Susan Bansgrove, Rick Morden, and Deborah van der Goes. It is young men and women such as these that encourage me in my conviction that the world is much safer in the hands of the newer generation than it ever was with those of my own older generation or of the generation between me and those former students.

Norman Pittenger

King's College
University of Cambridge
England

The Lure of Divine Love

PART ONE

Human Experience and Process Thought

1

A New Perspective

A

"Process thought is a way of looking on the world that provides promise for development. . . . It stresses reality as an organism, concepts as developing, and persons as becoming and perishing. Nothing is nailed down and yet there is continuity in the midst of flux. Even though one has not heard of Whitehead or Teilhard de Chardin, one finds that this kind of thinking makes sense of the world."

So writes American educator Randolph Crump Miller of Yale University in introducing a symposium (*Religious Education*, May-June 1973, p. 307). Perhaps his words are as good as any for summarizing the position taken by process thinkers in many parts of the world. Here, he says, is (a) a way of looking at the world, concerned (b) with development and (c) an organic or a societal view of things, which also recognizes (d) that concepts or ideas are not unchangeable and finds (e) that human personality is a "becoming" rather than some static essence. Finally, and perhaps most significantly, he notes (f) that while such a conceptuality sees the world in movement, there is still genuine "continuity in the midst of flux."

Those six points indicate in a very general way what process thinking is all about. They need to be spelled out, however, if the ordinary educated person is to grasp what they are trying to tell us. This I shall attempt to do in later sections of this introductory chapter. But some preliminary comments may be useful.

The process conceptuality has drawn much interest in our own day for many reasons, but perhaps its major attraction has been that it makes sense of the kind of world that modern scientific inquiry has disclosed, while at the same time taking seriously the depths of human experience with which the humanities, the religious outlook, and the aesthetic enterprise in its various expressions are conceived.

The insights of process thought have been found valuable in many different areas. For example, we shall see that this way of looking at the world has provided a helpful perspective in the theory and practice of education. So also in scientific inquiry, where process thought offers a position that accepts a mechanistic methodology but recognizes life and spirit. Recent thinking about aesthetics has benefited by the emphasis of process thought on feeling-tones, with their uniting of objectivity and subjectivity in a pattern of contrasts. Writers on ethical theory and problems of morality have been helped by the process insistence on human "becoming." Finally, an increasing number of Christian and Jewish theologians have used the insights of process thinkers to develop a way of reconceiving basic religious faith and its affirmations.

In my opinion the most important contributions that the process school has made to contemporary thought are (1) its deepening of our understanding of what it means to be human, including in that understanding the central place of sexuality in human existence, and (2) the remarkable assistance this conceptuality can give in our effort to rethink the basic religious issues of God, nature, and how God works in the world. It is here that the process stress upon becoming and upon persuasion or love as our chief clue both to God's nature and to human life is so instructive.

4

But process thinking is not concerned only with religion. It has a much wider spread, as we shall see. It is also closely related to other contemporary movements of thought, such as existentialism, the newer view of history, and psychological study, although it is not identical with any of them. Surely a comprehensive way of looking at the world, with an emphasis on dynamic development, interrelationship, and persuasion or love, can have considerable influence in many areas of experience. Above all, it can be illuminating in its contribution to the sense of human significance, and thus it can give some grounding for our feeling that life is worth living. Let us turn first to this human sense of life's value.

Most men and women assume that life is worth living, that it does have meaning, and that somehow the cosmos plays a part in providing this meaning. Is this claim absurd? I do not think so, and for the following reason.

When a writer like Jean-Paul Sartre declares that the only value of existence is in what we ourselves read into it, he fails to take account of a crucial point to which Gabriel Marcel, another French dramatist and philosopher, insistently called attention—the fact that the cosmos, the environment in which we have our existence, *permits* us to read meaning into life. Marcel puts this quite simply, recalling, for instance, that we make promises and intend to keep them and that thus the world is a place where making promises and intending to keep them is a genuine possibility. It is even more significant, he says, that promise-making is not only a possibility but also continually taking place. Moreover, ours is a world in which relationships are a given reality which nobody, not even a Sartre, can avoid. This world is very different from one in which such relationships would be impossible and in which the promising that accompanies them would seem absurd and unprofitable. For Marcel, to speak in this way about human existence and the world is not to indulge in airy and fruitless speculation but to affirm what we all know and experience. To deny it is to fall victim to the strange tendency of very learned people to talk nonsense about what everybody understands, even if not everybody can state it in convincing concepts or ideas.

This persistent sense of life's significance can be illustrated in yet another way. Let us suppose that a woman decides to commit suicide because at the moment she thinks that her existence is pointless. What then does she assume that her suicide will accomplish? Presuming that she is not mentally disturbed, she is convinced that somehow it is *worthwhile* to end her miserable and pointless life. In the very rejecting of significance on one level, she is asserting it on another—and on a deeper one too.

Many years ago a friend from my school days came to see me after a long period when we had not even been corresponding. He told me that he had decided to end his life and asked me if I could see any reason why he should not do this. I remembered that a psychiatrist had once told me that the best way to dissuade someone from suicide often is to appear to agree with the plan, so I replied that probably he would be right enough to do what he intended. This was a risky response, I know, but my friend, thus challenged as to the value of his own life, spent several hours listing for me all the reasons against his committing suicide. It was clear that underneath his sense of futility there was a deeper feeling of meaning which had been hidden or suppressed or pushed out of sight by his present worries. My friend went away, not to jump into the river as he had proposed but to return to his wife from whom he had been estranged, to take up his work once again, and eventually to become a well-known writer on scientific matters for a weekly journal.

However one might interpret such extreme cases, it is surely true that most people do find life worth living. In spite of boredom, drabness, loneliness, and futility, they wish to continue living. Modern existentialists speak of this enduring sense of meaning even when, like Sartre, they think it is a delusion. All high religion has the same insistence. The humanism that wishes to deny cosmic importance to human existence must still look at it in a cosmic setting, which in some strange way either itself gives meaning or is believed to be able to bear having meaning found in it. Process thinking asks us to take this existentialist feeling of significance seriously and analyze its various aspects, see how they fit into the world situation, generalize from them, and discover how they are related to what observation of the world discloses. In this fashion it complements the introspective look of the existentialist by speaking of a wider context. It asks what it really means to feel human and to act in a human manner, and to feel and act like this in a world like ours.

B

We must now say something about the development of the process conceptuality.

Process thought had its origin during the latter part of the nineteenth century in the increasing awareness that we live in an evolutionary world. Thinkers in many countries had become discontented both with a fixed and static picture of things, on the one hand, and with a purely mechanical interpretation of the evident fact of change, on the other. They believed that there was more to the creation than matter in motion. The very fact of motion, coupled with the deliverances of observation and experiment, revealed a *dynamic* kind of change. Hence in Great Britain men like Samuel Alexander (*Space, Time, and Deity*), Conway Lloyd-Morgan (in *Emergent Evolution* and *Life, Mind, and Spirit*), and Jan Smuts (in *Holism and Evolution*) began in the first decades of the twentieth century to work out a general philosophy which would take with great seriousness the total dynamic and evolutionary perspective. With this perspective they coupled an insistence on the interpenetrative or relational way in which the world goes on. But it was Alfred North Whitehead who developed most fully and carefully the principles of a genuinely processive view of things.

A mathematician at Trinity College in Cambridge, England, Whitehead had cooperated with his former student Bertrand Russell in the famous *Principia Mathematica*, but he had come to believe that the science with which he was familiar required a philosophical setting and interpretation. During his last years in Cambridge, he began work in this direction and continued it when he went to London to lecture at the Imperial College of Science and Technology. It was not until the mid-twenties of this century, however, that he set himself the task of thinking through, and then writing down, his conclusions. What finally emerged was a full-length sketch—not a *system*, he said, but a "vision of reality" —in which due account was taken of the newer way of looking at and understanding the world.

During Whitehead's last years, the American literary critic Edmund Wilson wrote an essay in which he spoke of Whitehead's incisive mind, constructive ability, keen insight, and openness to aesthetic values, combined with his awareness of scientific knowledge. To Wilson, Whitehead was the most important figure in contemporary thought. Unfortunately, Whitehead's style of writing did not make for easy reading, and even with such commendation as Wilson's his books were known during his lifetime only to professional philosophers, scientists, and a few persons of letters. Yet such works as *Science and the Modern World* (1925), the Edinburgh Gifford Lectures entitled *Process and Reality* (1929), and *Adventures of Ideas* (1933) were original and penetrating works, opening up new possibilities for thought in setting out an organic, or holistic, view of the world. Other works included *The Function of Reason* (1929), *Religion in the Making* (1926), *Symbolism: Its Meaning and Effect* (1927), and *The Aims of Education and Other Essays* (1929). Along with these, a collection of Whitehead's essays, *Essays in Science and Philosophy* (1947) dealt with the philosophical issues that science raises for the inquiring mind. Lectures given at Wellesley College and the University of Chicago, brought together and published under the title *Modes of Thought* (1938), are simpler in style and probably provide the best introduction to what

Whitehead was trying to say as the result of his deep reflection and his extraordinary range of knowledge in the sciences, art, literature, and ethical and religious matters.

In *Modes of Thought* there is a sentence that gives the key to Whitehead's thinking and helps us grasp why the process conceptuality, which owes so much to him, has its relevance for us today. Here is the sentence: "The key notion from which such construction [of a world view that takes into account the full richness of human experience] should start is that the energetic activity considered in physics is the emotional intensity entertained in life" (pp. 231-32).

What did Whitehead intend by these cryptic words? Essentially, that in a world such as ours, with creatures such as we feel ourselves to be in our moments of sensitive awareness, there is an intimate linkage between the thrust of human existence toward the achievement of goals and the creative movement of the cosmic order in its evolutionary drive. In other words, life—and above all humanly experienced life—belongs to and is part of the natural world. Life —and above all human life—cannot be rightly understood apart from that natural world. Neither can the natural world be rightly understood apart from life and above all human life. That life of ours is part of the cosmic process, and the ground of the cosmic process is thereby disclosed in some fashion in what human experience tells us. Conversely, at the same time, the cosmic process from which we have emerged and in which we exist cannot be properly grasped and described unless that experience is taken as a significant clue to what is really going on.

This is to say that the emotional intensity which gives human existence its peculiar quality is a manifestation of the energetic activity with which the natural sciences concern themselves. There can be no "false disjunction," in Whitehead's phrase, between the two. We belong in and to the world; and from the other side, what that world is like, what is happening in it, and whatever it may be said to mean are given concrete and particular expression in our own vivid and vital existence. A unified world view should make possible a coherent and consistent grasp of life *and* of nature, of human life *and* of the world.

We have only to read Lucien Price's fascinating reporting of conversations with Whitehead during the latter's last years in the American Cambridge to see that Whitehead was a remarkable example of a universal man who could propose and defend such a united world view. He lived deeply, vividly, and with zest. He was open to influence from every quarter —scientific, literary, artistic, musical, religious, and personal. He was not content with superficial appearances but sought the "depths of things." Indeed, Price tells us that a few days before his death in 1947 Whitehead spoke of human beings as "partakers of the creative process" who can find their "true destiny" only in seeing themselves as "co-creators in the universe" (*Dialogues of Alfred North Whitehead*, Mentor ed., 1956, p. 297). In several essays that he contributed in his later years to *The Atlantic Monthly*, Whitehead again illustrated the point, showing how the place where one lives, one's environment and one's friends, one's challenges and risks, one's problems and difficulties, as well as the moments of one's joy and exaltation, are instrumental in making one what one is. He also showed how all this may be seen as the manifestation of the basic cosmic structure and dynamic.

Whitehead's insight, grounded as it was in deep experience and reflection and confirmed by experiment and observation, grasped human existence as organic to the universe. Much early religion had made that existence the great exception to everything else; much modern science had talked in the same way. But Whitehead was convinced that the only way to make intelligible the meaning or significance which we naturally take for granted in our ordinary moments is to relate our concrete experience as a human being to the mystery of the dynamic evolutionary process that is going on around us *and in us*. Human existence is indeed distinctive, yet it is not separated from everything else. It has its own qualities and capabilities, but these are not without analogues elsewhere. *We belong to the world that has produced us.* Hence, anything that deepens self-awareness contributes to our knowledge of that world, and anything that increases our knowledge of the world contributes to our self-understanding.

In this comprehensive view of things, static concepts are inevitably ruled out as mistaken abstractions. Historically, we humans have frequently hankered after absolutely fixed truths, utterly final positions, unchanging and unchangeable notions—everything that Paul Elmer More summed up when he spoke of the pursuit of "the demon of the absolute." But we cannot have these things, for the world is not like that, nor are we ourselves finished articles who can be described or defined in terms that admit of no alteration. As a matter of fact, nobody has ever really been able to rest in such a view. Whether we like it or not, we do not remain in one stay; neither does our world. As Whitehead put it, "the reality *is* the process." Once we have arrived, we find ourselves off on a new journey, for despite the famous words of Shakespeare, time does *not* "have a stop," and neither do we.

C

Once we have accepted the world and ourselves in this new way, there are two important practical consequences. One is the possibility of a vision of things that preserves their richness, variety, and freshness, while at the same time recognizing the continuities that persist through all these. The other is the importance of decision in determining how things will go in the future. Each of these consequences must now receive our attention.

Two familiar poems by the American poet Robert Frost help us here. In his poem "Mending Wall," Frost spoke of "something . . . that doesn't love a wall, / That wants it down." Dividing up the world may be useful and important for this or that academic discipline or for convenience in handling a particular problem, but when we try to make sense of existence it simply will not do. Then we see that walls, however carefully built and however necessary to preserve concrete integrity, are bound to collapse. Specialization or compartmentalizing will not serve us in the long run, no matter how helpful they may be in the short run.

In the other poem, "The Road Not Taken," Frost tells how one evening at a crossroads he was faced with having to choose the road to follow. The road he chose, he says, "has made all the difference." Here we have the inescapable requirement for decision, and with it the point that decisions do make a difference. "They have consequences," as Whitehead once remarked to a student. Things can never be the same once a choice has been made.

Process thinking assumes that everything contributes to make a unity of some sort, that we have to do with cosmos not chaos, with order not anarchy. It is clear to most of us that the day is long past when anyone could hope to have the total knowledge that may have been possible in an earlier age. The vast accumulation of information and the need for developing special skills make it impossible to possess more than a very partial and limited grasp of "things entire." Yet when this patent fact is pushed to extreme limits, it can and has produced a fragmentation of human existence and an incapacity to entertain a synoptic view of things. We have heard that physicians nowadays tend to treat a kidney or a liver, not a patient. The sense of wholeness has diminished, and as a result we feel we are less than full persons and we see our world as an assemblage of disparate and unrelated entities.

The process perspective changes this. Not only does it *assume* that there is cosmos and not chaos, but it is also concerned to *show* that this is the case. It does this by investigating human experience and the natural order in which that experience is had. The result is the vision of a unity between human existence and the world order, even if there is a real distinction between the two. Of course, none of us can know everything and fit everything together. Yet we can have the vision of such a patterning, and it is this vision that process thought provides for us.

This is true also with respect to the importance of decision. Very often it does not seem that the choices we make can really change things. Sometimes it seems that we cannot make significant decisions of any sort, for we seem to be very much creatures of circumstance, determined by heredity or environment or both. This can lead to a pessimism that denies any significant sense of responsibility. After all, we may ask, are we not helpless in the face of relentless forces that take no account of us and that we can do nothing to alter? People who are led to adopt this position feel they have lost their dignity; they are adrift on a sea of futility. Process thought, however, insists that we *can* decide and that our decisions *do* make a difference. Moreover, that insistence does not require us to believe that supernatural interventions break into the world from outside, nor does it require us to deny the genuine continuities we know so well. On the contrary, from its study of human experience, and from its observation of the order of nature, process thought is able to discern a pattern of decision that reaches down to the lowest level of the creation and up to fully conscious human choice—even up to deity itself, for that matter.

How is this? We might start by looking at the word itself. "Decision" is derived from the Latin *decidere*, "to cut off." A quantum of energy *decides* in this sense, for it moves *here*, not *there*, thus "cutting off" one of its possible moves. In this instance of energy events of an apparently simple sort (yet really not so simple, as modern physics tell us), there is something analogous to decision as we ourselves experience it. Of course, quanta do not make conscious choices among or between alternatives, but we assume that *we* do. But if there is a degree of decision-making, however primitive, at that lowest level there is a probability that at other more complex and developed levels decision of a higher type will be found. As an alternative, when we look into ourselves and recognize our awareness of choices made, we may claim that we are given a clue to a pattern running through the world as a whole, precisely because people are part of that world, emerge from it, and are not complete exceptions to it. This is a world, we recall, where "energetic activity" and "emotional intensity" are not discontinuous but are mutually related and mutually involved.

So much for the vision of wholeness and the reality of decision and its consequences. Process thought has other contributions of a very practical sort. Let us look at two of them: the question of the "two cultures" and the question of "the religious and the secular."

Lord Snow once gave a famous lecture on the two cultures, one scientific and the other humanistic. In that lecture he expressed grave concern about the way in which the two seemed increasingly alien one to the other, so that the scientist cannot comprehend the humanities, and the classical scholar or literary critic cannot understand the scientific way of thinking. Yet both, he said, are genuine elements in human life. The person who is nothing but a scientist is missing much that is valuable, and the humanist who lives only in terms of aesthetic sensibility is also missing a vastly important area of human study and experience.

Process thought's emphasis on wholeness—its recognition of the aesthetic *and* the scientific, of feeling-tones as well as precise observation and experiment—helps to hold together these two different but not ultimately contradictory ways of thinking, living, and acting. The detailed exactness of scientific reporting and technological competence, on the one hand, and the deeply felt sense of value, with its appreciative and emotional stress, on the other hand, can be grasped together even if we cannot work out completely and fully their proper relationship.

There is much talk about "the religious" as contrasted with "the secular." How is each to be understood, and how are they related? We seem to demand, and wish to express, a yearning for a reference beyond self and nature that will make sense of our immediate experience. We are aware of what Tillich called "the sacred," possessed by what he styled an "ultimate concern" that gives meaning and significance to all we say and do. We may not think in traditionally religious terms; we may reject conventional religious ideas. But a sense of the transcendent, unexhausted in our immediacies and mysteriously beckoning us toward ultimacies, seems to be part of the human makeup.

At the same time, we know that we have "come of age," to use Dietrich Bonhoeffer's oft-quoted phrase. We are convinced that we live in a world where we can do much to provide what is needed and to know what is to be known. We do not believe any longer in divine intrusions or miraculous deliverances from the situations into which we have gotten ourselves. We cannot revert to the time when people thought that some power or person will come in from outside to take care of us when we are in difficulty or extricate us from having to choose this or that way forward. So it has seemed to many that there is an irremediable conflict between the religious and the secular. There is a giving up of one for the sake of the other, or there is a compartmentalizing of existence in which one side leaves the other entirely alone.

But if the "energetic activity" in the cosmos is indeed disclosed to us in the "emotional intensity" of lived experience, if the way things go is determined by some agency that does not occasionally interfere but rather "makes things make themselves"—as the French philosopher Lequier put it long ago—if this is the case, then the reality and value of the secular can be preserved while at the same time the deepest religious insight with respect to the "more," the "transcendent," "ultimate concern," and a "reference beyond oneself" can also be given due recognition. Above all, we may come to understand cosmic "refreshment and companionship," which Whitehead once said religion in its practical aspect is all about. The deepest yearning and satisfaction in us expressed "religiously" is not then contradicted by our awareness that we have responsibility in a "secular" way for what we make of ourselves and our society, not to mention the more recently recognized need for responsibility for the way in which, for good or for ill, we use natural resources and contribute to the future of the world in its ecological structure.

D

What is the procedure followed by process thinkers in establishing their broad interpretation of things? How does this differ from the older type of metaphysical inquiry that for a great many people, perhaps especially in English-speaking lands, seems to be nothing more than speculation with little basis in fact?

In that older mode of metaphysics, the purpose was to arrive at conclusions that were taken as omni-competent and all-inclusive in the sense that some universal scheme could provide the answer to all the questions people might ask. By a process of reasoning which was usually deductive rather than inductive—that is, starting from general principles assumed to be true rather than from a study of concrete phenomena—it was believed that we could demonstrate a first cause or self-existent reality or self-contained being or unmoved mover. Or if a start was made from the world we know, the procedure was to argue from the supposedly clear evidence of design or the fact of creaturely contingency toward a conclusion that indicated a designer or purposer who explained anything and everything "without remainder," or toward a necessary being that was in no way dependent upon anything else.

Whatever the type of logic and argument, one assumption was simply taken for granted by almost every metaphysical thinker in the old style: the Greek conception of perfection as total immutability or changelessness. Movement, alteration, development, and the like were thought to be somehow less perfect, less good, and less real than a being or a principle that was self-contained, self-existent, without essential relations to and without dependence upon the created world. We might sum it up by saying that the intention was to arrive at an "Absolute," however portrayed, which would explain everything. And for most thinkers this Absolute was thought to be mental or spiritual, although one school of thought was prepared to endorse a basic reality of materialistic type.

During the last half-century this kind of philosophical procedure has been attacked by the increasingly influential school of linguistic and analytic philosophers. In one way or another, followers of that school tell us that we have neither the data nor the methods to engage meaningfully in such extrapolations, whether from speculation, human experience, or observation of the world. They are sure that no verification of these conclusions is possible. Their truth or falsehood cannot be decided.

Process thought does not concede the linguistic or analytical claim that no verification of a world vision is possible from experience or observation. Members of the process school have attacked the positivistic restriction of meaningful statements to tautological propositions (which simply repeat in the conclusion what is already found in the premises) or to experimentally demonstrable ones (such as are possible in scientific work). They are convinced that such narrowing of meaningful discourse is arbitrary and selective and that it rests upon implicit metaphysical presuppositions which themselves are never subjected to critical examination. Furthermore, this narrowing is a denial of what we all take for granted.

But the process thinker does not work in the way that earlier metaphysical construction did. Whitehead himself said the process method was like an aviator who takes off from a well-known place, makes the flight, and then returns to earth where once again he is with things that he knows from his own experience. During the flight the aviator looks to see if what he observes from above either confirms or denies the notions with which he began. On returning, the aviator checks again to see if those notions are still as near as can be to the observed facts.

In other words, process thinkers start from experience, more particularly the deeply intuited awareness of what happens in human existence. They make generalizations that may be more widely applicable. These are referred to the various areas of experience and observation open to inspection to see if they will fit, if they will help make sense of those areas and provide useful interpretative principles. If they do not fit, process thinkers know that the generalizations are in error. If they do fit, even though there may be loose ends and ambiguities, it will be an assurance that so far they are indicative of how things go in the world. Process thinkers do not engage in flights into the sheerly unknown or indulge in abstract speculation that has no grounding in experience or experiment or observed data. They generalize from what is known, and they always return to a consideration of evidence that will confirm or contradict the generalized principles.

Moreover, process thinkers do not assume that their conclusions, whatever they may be, can ever be entirely conclusive. On the contrary, they stress that all human approach to truth is tentative, since it is bound to lack the complete clarity we would like to have. It is subject to correction, modification, and change, but since thought must proceed on *some* principles, process thinkers are prepared to trust those they have reached and to test them in as many fields as possible. This whole procedure has been well styled "metaphysics in a new mode."

In this approach, full recognition is given to the dynamic quality of experience, the interrelated or societal quality of life, the significance of decisive action, and the appreciative or valuational side of things, quite as much as to the regularities observed in the creation and the elements of order and patterning seen there. But the start is from our own human awareness of how things go with us. We have no other place to start, since this is the one area with which we are acquainted firsthand. With everything else we have but second-hand acquaintance, however trustworthy that may seem to us.

Let us now consider what human experience tells us. We know that we are living, dynamic creatures who are "becoming," in that to a greater or lesser degree we are fulfilling potentialities. We know that we are intimately related with others of the human race and that in some mysterious fashion we fit into and are part of the natural order. We know that we are yearning, desiring, striving creatures, seeking goals which constitute what may properly be called our "subjective aim" but which we also know have been given to us in the very fact of our coming into existence. We know the experience of love, with its joy and its anguish, its ecstasy and its agony. We know that we are capable of some degree of rational inquiry and thought, but even more significantly of appreciation and aesthetic delight. We know that we are affected and influenced by what goes on around us and makes its impact on us. More particularly we know the persuasive power of loving concern, which is so much stronger than the coercive force that can indeed make us go through the motions of acceptance and conformity but can never bring us to a freely given assent that involves all our personality. Finally, we know ourselves to be creatures who make decisions, who can and do make choices, however limited the areas in which this is possible may be. And we know that these choices have their consequences, for which we are prepared to assume a measure of responsibility.

Suppose we begin with what we deeply feel ourselves to be. If human experience is indeed organic with the natural order in its ongoing movement, should we not be prepared to use this experience to illuminate for us what that order is like and how it goes? And if we do this, may we not rightly use the generalizations drawn from that experience, taking them to be indicative of the fundamental dynamic and structure of the totality of things? Everything we know can make its contribution: our scientific knowledge as well as our aesthetic valuing, our sense of moral responsibility as well as our technical competence, our yearning for transcendence as well as our occasional awareness of a "dearest freshness deep down things" (in G.M. Hopkins' lovely phrase) and of some companionship greater than, but mediated through, our human friendship and love.

To those who accept the general process conceptuality, this full and rich human experience is the starting place, the only one we know intimately and personally. Yet it is a way into other areas of the world's ongoing. It seems to be in accordance with them, despite the terrifying presence of evil and the obvious contradictions seen in so many places. It makes possible a synoptic vision that redeems life from triviality and absurdity. Of course, the confidence that results is not demonstrable in strict logic or by exact scientific tests. But to think that living truth could be demonstrated in that way would itself be absurd and trivializing.

Where do we come out? We come out at a vision of reality in which there is dynamic movement, with a societal or interrelational quality that pervades the whole, and with a genuine place for decisions that count. We come out with a recognition that the basic constituents seen in that vision are not *things,* fixed entities shuffled about in this way or that, but rather "energy events," instances of "energetic activity" and "emotional intensity." This is the kind of world which surrounds us and of which we are a part.

The stress upon persuasion or love tells us something else too. While coercion or force is indeed plainly present in the world, it is ultimately neither so effective nor so persistent as the persuasive element, the love that is at work in men and women and, they dare to add, in the world. The vision finds its center here, and we shall return again and again to it.

This stress does not overlook or deny the appalling fact of evil in the world. But evil is not a radical distortion of the whole structure of things; rather, it is refusal to move forward, a continuing existence in backwaters or in narrowly selfish sidelines, a rejection of better possibilities and the choice of nonshareable possibilities. It is to some extent the inevitable result of conflicts that come from the varied decisions the constituent energy events are enabled to make. At the human level, moral evil is essentially a disregard of others and a falsely self-centered preference for immediate gains or pleasures without respect for the common good. And sin—to use the religious word for the most serious defect in human experience—is not a breaking of regulations or laws imposed from outside but a violation of the solicitation and lure of love, a willingness to rest content with what seems to satisfy human striving but what in plain fact damages relationships at every level: with the deepest self, with others of our kind, with the world of nature, and with the cosmic thrust of love, or God.

I close this chapter with a renewed invitation to consider the emphasis on love or persuasion that is so central to process thinking. When Thornton Wilder ended his novel *The Bridge of San Luis Rey* with the words "Love is the only survival, the only meaning," he was speaking like a process thinker. But process thinkers are not the only ones who have spoken like this. For example, my fellow Kingsman of an earlier generation, G. Lowes Dickinson, whose general philosophical position was quite different, could write thus in his book *After Two Thousand Years:*

> The whole universe groans and travails together to accomplish a purpose more august than you can divine; and of that your guesses at good and evil are but wavering symbols. Yet dark though night may be and stumbling your step, your hand is upon the clue. Nourish then your imagination, strengthen your will, and purify your love. For what your imagination anticipates shall be achieved, what will pursues will be done, and what love seeks shall be revealed.

E.M. Forster, quoting these words in his biography *Goldsworthy Lowes Dickinson* (Harcourt Brace Jovanovich, 1973, p. 204), spoke of them as "splendid in diction, warm in emotion, and filled with wisdom," which they are indeed.

For Dickinson their origin was in Plato who in the *Symposium,* the *Phaedrus,* and the *Timaeus* spoke in precisely this vein. But as Whitehead remarked, "what Plato discerned in theory," with his insistence on "the victory of persuasion over force," was confirmed "in act" by what Whitehead called the "Galilean vision." In a genuinely human life, that of Jesus of Nazareth, love was disclosed both as sharing suffering and achieving "supreme victory." And the disclosure in Jesus does not stand alone. In one way or another, the persisting religious vision of humankind in all places has moved in this direction, toward an interpretation of "reality" as a dynamic process in which persuasion overcomes sheer force. Professor Trevor Ling has recently demonstrated that Gautama, the writer of the *Bhagavad-Gita,* the Islamic Sufis, Lao-Tze, Confucius, and others have arrived at this vision too. In his carefully documented work *Religion of East and West* he remarks that at this point, if not at others, there is an extraordinary religious consensus. Process thinkers are prepared to accept that consensus as indicative of something very deep in the structure of the world, not as mere human wish fulfillment but as the way in which (despite so much that appears contradictory and negative) things really do go.

2

The Humanities and the Arts

The founder of process thought in its generally accepted version was, as we have noted, Alfred North Whitehead. He was an English mathematician and theoretical physicist, who ended his academic career lecturing in philosophy in the United States. The son of a parson-schoolmaster in the Isle of Thanet in Kent, in the southeastern part of England, Whitehead attended Sherborne School in Dorset, one of England's oldest schools for boys; he then went to Cambridge University as an undergraduate at Trinity College, which had been founded by King Henry VIII. There he remained for more than a quarter of a century after graduating and being elected a fellow of his college. He became lecturer in mathematics in the university and a distinguished member of the academic community. Bertrand Russell was among his pupils, and he had many other close friends in all the faculties. Yet Whitehead left Cambridge and joined the faculty of the University of London. He lectured at the Imperial Institute of Science and Technology, and while there he served as head of the senate of that university and had much to do with the revision of the curriculum and with teaching methods, as well as with extramural education, taking a special interest in workers' education. Finally, just as he was planning retirement, Whitehead was invited to Harvard University in the United States. There he lectured in philosophy for more than a decade. After retiring from his professorship he produced some of his major works, and he and his wife continued to live in Cambridge, Massachusetts, until his death in 1947 at the age of eighty-seven.

Whitehead's major interest during much of his life and certainly until he went to the United States, had been in the sciences, particularly in mathematics and the mathematical side of physics. But from his earliest days, as he recalled toward the end of his life, he had been a great reader, especially of poetry and fiction. As a boy, he had been taught both Latin and Greek, as was common for young people of his background and class. He was familiar with religion and had respected and admired his father's devout and genuine faith. When he married, his wife brought into his life an even deeper interest in the humanities and in art, not least in music. She was a woman of aesthetic sensitivity, and she made him understand (as he himself said), that an awareness of beauty of form, sound, and color is very much in the center of a truly human experience. Finally, Whitehead had always been conscious of, and had given time and attention to, ethical issues, not only pondering questions of personal human responsibility but also being active in the realm of political and economic affairs; indeed, he took part time and again in English political campaigns, on the liberal and labor side because of his deep concern for social justice.

I have outlined Whitehead's varied interests to enable us to see that the man who developed the basic categories of process thinking was not a narrow specialist but a man of deep culture and wide sympathies—truly a humanist. It has been said that Whitehead was one of the really "universal" people of recent years, with much more than a superficial acquaintance with the best that has been thought and said in human history and at the same time with a sympathetic concern for many areas and aspects of contemporary life. Indeed, he has been more than just the founder of process thought. For those who have adopted that conceptuality, his breadth of interest and his openness to all sorts of human experience have also been a model to follow.

But it is not only Whitehead's own example that has brought adherents of process thought to their concern for the humanities and the arts as much as for science and formal philosophy. The process perspective is itself an invitation to take these with enjoyment and to recognize their importance. This is because process thought is concerned with analyzing human experience at its deepest and widest, never being content with regarding that experience abstractly but always intent on its concrete disclosure to us of what it means and what it feels like to be human—to be human in a world that is both the origin of and the setting for human existence with its distinctive qualities and capacities.

A book that seeks to present the process conceptuality should devote a chapter to considering some ways in which process thinking illuminates the humanistic disciplines, especially the way these disciplines invite men and women to participate, to find enjoyment in that participation, and in the end to experience an enrichment of their own lives—to know what Whitehead called a heightening of the "emotional intensity" which, as we have noted, was for him important for its own sake but which has the added value of suggesting to us a more profound understanding of the "energetic activity" found in the wider cosmos itself.

In a conversation some friends had with Whitehead's American interpreter Charles Hartshorne not long ago, that process thinker, who was approaching his eighties at the time, made this comment: "If I were bringing up a child, I should not start by burdening him with a lot of moral rules. I should begin by trying to help the child see that life can be beautiful and can be lived beautifully. Then I should not need to bother so much about how moral ideas would develop." This remark sums up very precisely and movingly the point I shall be making in this chapter.

Life can be beautiful, and life can be lived beautifully. What does this mean? A great many people will say that it is only a bit of sentimental talk which need not be taken seriously. Their saying this is an indication of the superficiality of much modern thinking and, consequently, much modern living.

The frequent reduction of beauty to the merely pretty, the notion that it is sentimental to delight in the aesthetic side of experience, the easy dismissal of that aesthetic component of human existence as either irrelevant or unimportant, and the resulting willingness to acquiesce in ugliness—all these are proof of the cheapness and triviality so prevalent among us. It is tragic that people who should know better, men and women of excellent education and background, are so often prepared to accept this attitude. Even in academic circles one frequently finds a contempt for art, a dismissal of the aesthetic as interesting only to those who happen to "like that sort of thing," and a refusal to consider the aesthetic experience in *all* its aspects as a clue to something very deep and real in human life and in the world in which we live.

On the other hand, I know a considerable number of distinguished scientists who are keenly sensitive to the aesthetic, not only because they take "elegance" to be one of the criteria for a sound scientific theory but also because they have come to feel that without opening themselves to and developing within their lives some profound aesthetic awareness they would be greatly impoverished. Some of the "greatest" people I have known, whether distinguished scholars or quite ordinary people who yet have lived deeply and well, have shown just this sensitivity. I saw and met Whitehead only three times, but I had the privilege of a long friendship with Paul Tillich. Tillich was a man who delighted in art, especially in painting and music; who read widely, either in the original or in translation, in all the literature of the world; and whose sensitivity to the aesthetic was equaled only by a remarkable gift for logical thought. Furthermore, it is unquestionably a fact of our time that many younger people are returning to just such a concern, which explains the growing popularity among them of music, painting, sculpture, and the other arts. These young people, some of them spending most of their working hours in dull jobs, know very well that the aesthetic is for them a great release. But they know also that it makes life richer and finer. In a word, they see that life *can* be beautiful and *can* be lived beautifully, as Charles Hartshorne put it.

If process thinkers are to be loyal to the conceptuality they accept, they *must* take this attitude. The perspective that process thought provides includes the aesthetic as one of its data. We might phrase it even more strongly and say that in a sense it is the *basic* datum.

What then is the aesthetic? I have urged that it does not mean prettiness or a merely superficial emotional response. Neither is it only a matter of human subjectivity, although some unthinking people have argued that this is the case. If it were merely that, we should have to attribute to our own feelings the loveliness we see, or think we see, outside us. But, no. Most of us are certain that there is something objective about the truly beautiful. And this certainty, so deep in human sensibility, cannot be dismissed as irrelevant.

In process thinking, with its stress upon the profound relationship between human existence and the world which is that existence's origin and context, no dichotomy between subjectivity and objectivity is possible. All human knowledge is a matter of relationship between objective data of some sort—even if so badly ordered that the result is the concept of a nonexistent entity like a unicorn!—*and* a perceiving subject. This rules out the sort of philosophical idealism (better called "idea-ism" or "mentalism") that finds genuine knowledge and experience a purely subjective affair. It also rules out the phenomenalism that confines data to the external world and is unable to explain how we come to assume we *know* these data.

Now, if ordinary knowledge is a subjective-objective complex, then aesthetic awareness is equally, indeed supremely, subjective-objective. On the subjective side, the aesthetic—as the very word indicates, if we take account of its Greek derivation—is primarily the business of feeling, an imaginative grasp that is more penetrating than intellectual knowledge alone. Awareness of the aesthetic is a kind of sympathetic identification with the presented material. That material, which constitutes the objective side of the aesthetic situation, is essentially a patterning or ordering which harmonizes contrasts. It is in fact a formal arrangement that satisfies the observer or listener or participant. Thomas Aquinas said that beauty is "clarity of form"—a shining forth of pattern that evokes a positive response of appreciation. Whitehead's view was very similar.

When we contemplate or read or hear something that we describe as beautiful, we find ourselves both stimulated and given a sense of harmony. There is excitement and fulfillment or satisfaction. In Whitehead's own words, there is zest and peace. The zest is not disturbing, as if it entirely disrupted the sensibility of the participant in the experience, but the peace is not mere passivity. On the contrary, the two belong together and modify each other. The zest gives deep contentment, and the peace is a felt union of the experience with the experient, who feels genuine fulfillment and great enrichment through the intensifying of the emotions.

This is not irrational. When imaginative awareness— what in some discussions is called empathy, or a sensitive subjective entrance into the presented objective reality—is entirely contradictory to all reason and becomes *nothing more* than emotionalism, we have only fantasy. That is how Samuel Taylor Coleridge put it. Coleridge was quite clear about the distinction between imagination as the reason of the total personality, which includes but surpasses ratiocination, and fantasy or mere imagining, which belongs to the realm of the unreal and fanciful. A total concentration upon rationality alone, in its narrower sense of syllogistic reasoning or the simple reporting of experiment and observation, can produce the type of person who has lost awareness of the "more" in human experience, of the unexplained and unexplored, of the mysterious depths and heights that give human life its vivacity and its color. Dean Inge of St. Paul's in London spoke once of imagination as "reason with wings." Perhaps that was too high-flown a definition, but it makes the point.

No human life can be complete if the aesthetic side is neglected or denied. Hence, for example, during their education young people ought to be exposed to the beautiful in all its aspects, and it is tragic that this is not sufficiently recognized. The houses in which people live, the furnishings they contain, the towns where those houses are located, the surrounding countryside with its natural beauty—all these can express dignity and serve as patterned structures that are not only functional but also lovely to contemplate. The spoliation of the countryside, the ugliness of our cities, and the senseless ornamentation of public and private places are all examples of serious failure in aesthetic sensitivity. So also is the vulgarity of much writing, drama, cinema production, and music. To say this is not to deny the need for relevance, nor is it a call for censorship or suppression by official agencies. Neither is it to ask for a "prettying up," since that would be to fall once again into cheap vulgarity, like the overdecoration and sentimentalizing so often found when people make an effort without any education in art to escape from the drabness and dullness of their daily work. We need training in genuine aesthetic appreciation, and I agree with Sir Herbert Read that such training in art should be a part of genuine education.

All this is a natural consequence of the process way of looking at ourselves and our world. It is the result of grasping the wholeness of things, the many-sidedness of human existence, and the need for complementing functional efficiency by joy in doing and speaking and living. Above all, it seeks for the satisfaction that comes from the fulfilling of humankind's yearning for harmony or peace. Peace, yes, but as I urged above, peace of the sort that allows zest, adventure, and intensity of experience full play.

Another point should be made here. One of the richest sources for our grasp of what it means to be human is found in the literature, music, and art we have inherited from the past. Without some acquaintance with this inheritance we are likely to be victims of the merely contemporary. Process thought teaches that the past is important because it provides us with the materials upon which present decisions may rightly be made, materials which are in vital continuity with the age-long movement in the world from the past into the future. We are not asked to *confine* ourselves to the past; in that case, the aesthetic would be nothing more than repetition. But we should not confine ourselves to the present either, for if we do that we are denying ourselves the heritage our ancestors have given us and their insight into human motivation, desire, sensibility, appreciation, and understanding. In a truly whole world past and present go together. The continuities are to be such that opportunity for new experiments, new modes of writing and painting and composing, will not be without foundation in the persistent aesthetic experience of the human race. The truly aesthetic, then, is not mere archaeology, nor does it reek of easy-going contemporaneity. Instead, it is a fusion of the past with present, and it opens up possibilities for the enrichment of life in the future.

This is not the place to explore the several media through which aesthetic sensitivity is manifested. They are indeed varied, and one or another will have its particular attraction to each of us. But I will single out one medium that has special appeal to me and can serve as a paradigm for the other equally important and valuable media. Music is the medium I find moving and enriching in my own experience.

Music has a quality that is not generally found: its incommunicability in any idiom other than itself. There is a familiar story about a celebrated pianist who, after he had completed his rendition of a piece of music, was asked, "What does that *mean*?" His answer was simple: "I will show you what it means." Then he played the piece again and said, "*That* is what it means."

The pianist gave the right answer to the question. Music is music. It *means* what it conveys through its combination of sounds. There is no way of stating that meaning by verbal chatter, and it cannot be defined, as some technicians have thought, by an analysis of the physics of music, the measurement of tones and the mathematical arrangement of notes. Music is *sui generis*. If you want to put it so, it is the supreme instance of art for art's sake. Presumably this is why many musicians are suspicious of "program music" which purports to paint some scene in tone or to articulate some idea through sound. Yet in another sense we might say that *all* music does paint scenes and convey ideas. The point is that the scenes painted in music are *musical* scenes and the ideas conveyed by it are *musical* ideas. With the inner ear the musician hears and feels and maybe even "sees"; then the musician composes the piece. The performing artist is grasped by what the composer has heard or felt or seen, and excellence as a performer is to be judged not only by how well the piece is executed but also by how well the performer communicates both the interpretation of the composer's intention and the personal experience deep inside. And the audience is caught up into this complex situation and becomes a participant in it.

Those who love music know that it conveys "thoughts that do often lie too deep for tears," thoughts that lie so deep that they are beyond articulation. Here is sheer beauty. Here is the union of activity and response. Here the listener's "emotional intensity" is heightened by an ordering of sounds that bring musical contrasts together in harmonious accord. Songs that have words can do this, of course, when the words and the music seem to be marvelously wedded, but so also can songs without words, music that is simply music, like a Mozart symphony or a Beethoven concerto or a work by Mahler or Bartok, Sibelius or Messiaen. In all these, music is an instance of what Clive Bell styled "significant form." But the form must not be intruded into the material, and the significance must not be spelled out in terms of some other medium.

Music speaks to the human heart *and* mind, the human emotions *and* understanding. Other media—the novel, the poem, the dance, the play, painting, sculpture, design—do much the same thing, each in its own distinctive manner. The end product is an enriching of human life as well as a deepening of our sense of what it is to be human at all. A process conceptuality finds place for all this and welcomes it; it also tells us that any genuine interpretation of the world and its way of going on must remember and give adequate expression to the enormous importance of the aesthetic as one of our clues, maybe the chiefest, to what *is* going on.

3

The Scientific Enterprise

I begin this chapter, a discussion of process thought's relevance for the scientific enterprise, with some hesitation. I am not a professional scientist, although for a brief time I studied chemistry as a major interest. But I am encouraged by many conversations with friends who *are* professional scientists, some of them distinguished men and women in their particular fields, who not only have provided me with considerable information but have confirmed my opinion that process thought offers a useful context for scientific observation and experiment by providing a perspective for the framing of hypotheses.

There was a time, especially in the middle of the nineteenth century, when those engaged in scientific work were inclined to look at the cosmos as a great machine, relentlessly and meaninglessly grinding along. Some historians of science have said that this attitude was the result of the primacy given to Newtonian physics, a primacy which continued for some two hundred years. With the evolutionary interpretation of the appearance of human beings, developed by Darwin and others, the position changed. There was a tendency to see the changes in the natural order, and everywhere else too, as similar to the reshuffling of a pack of cards or the redistribution of particles of matter. Hence we had the construction of philosophies of materialistic naturalism. Mind, spirit, human evaluation, and appreciation, the sense of freedom of choice, and the like were supposed to be merely epiphenomenal, like the steam of a locomotive, which does not make any real difference to the running of the engine. Everything was rigidly determined; little or no room was left for chance, for freedom, for purpose, or indeed for life.

Naturally, that outlook brought about a reaction. In its place some biologists, for example, suggested that each instance of living nature, more especially at the higher levels, was controlled by an entelechy, an invisible spiritual or mental agent. This was the vitalistic hypothesis associated especially with the German Hans Driesch but accepted by a number of other workers in the biological field. For various reasons, however, and chiefly because methodologically it was unnecessary, this view did not commend itself to most of those actually engaged in experimental work. They were convinced that one could get further and discover more by employing a mechanistic model for what even they felt obliged to call "living" phenomena.

Still another possible approach did not suggest the abandonment of mechanistic method but severely restricted its application. The mechanical aspect was there, to be sure, but it was relatively unimportant in the total picture. Thus there appeared the philosophy of creative evolution, whose leading protagonist was Henri Bergson, a French biologist who had turned to philosophical writing. Bergson said that the mechanical models resemble a "still" seen when a movie film has been stopped at a given point. But the reality is the *flow* of the film, while the "still" is only an abstraction that is misleading as to what the film is about. There is an invisible but ever present life-force, which he called the *élan vital,* running through everything; this is *the* reality. The mechanistic models are convenient and useful for special experimental purposes but not finally significant.

There were also scientists who succeeded in compartmentalizing their lives. When they were in the laboratory they were prepared to follow mechanistic methods to the very limit, but outside the laboratory and in other contexts they were eager to speak of mind, spirit, freedom, and God—yet without relating the two areas of concern. Such a compartmentalization was especially popular with strictly "biblicist Christians," since it enabled them to accept in one area what they rejected in another. For example, miracles are related in the Bible and are to be believed because they are recorded there, but they do not happen in any realm with which modern science is concerned. Such dichotomizing of thought and experience is logically impossible for anyone who grasps the unitary character of things, and above all if one accepts the evolutionary interpretation of the world. Nonetheless, it was—and occasionally still is—adopted.

The important event of the past century has been the complete collapse, save within a very limited field, of the older mechanistic scheme. Whitehead once pointed out that as a total picture of how the world goes classical Newtonian physics itself collapsed. Albert Einstein is often named as the person who brought about this collapse, but there were others before him and beside him. While still a fellow and a lecturer in mathematics at Trinity College in Cambridge, Whitehead told how he witnessed the breaking down of the Newtonian scheme in the nineties of the last century. Quantum physics, the principle of indeterminacy, relativity theory, and the like, were all instrumental in bringing about this change.

At the same time, a new approach was coming to the fore in the sciences that deal with living phenomena. Vitalism was not a possible view, but neither was the presumably omnicompetent mechanical scheme. In their place an organic (in Whitehead's word, "organismic") picture was found necessary to the newer understanding of evolution itself. Novelties did occur, but they occurred within the wider continuities of nature. Thus evolution was interpreted as epigenetic, as technical jargon put it; it was not merely or only the mechanical rearrangement of bits of matter.

The thinkers who adopted this view believed that because

novelty is real and inescapable the natural order should be characterized as basically a continuity in which, as we have just seen, genuinely new things emerge. The operational word here is emerge. Without any absolute break and without any intrusive introduction of external factors, nature can produce what hitherto has not been present. But how? The answer proposed was that the novelty is in ordering or patterning or arranging previous materials in such a way that a difference appears. The organic, interrelational, interdependent nature of things brings about the emergence of the new. Of course, in one sense potentiality for such novelty is present in the previous "stuff," but it cannot be made actual until the right new relationships are established among the various ingredients of the "stuff."

Nowhere is this seen so clearly as in the appearance of the human species. Below I shall quote at length from a distinguished scientist who has admirably summed up the qualities that differentiate human beings from the animals to which biologically they are related. At the moment, however, I wish to indicate—relying on the conversation of my scientific friends—the way in which elsewhere in the understanding of the cosmos a change has taken place. This is found in the study of quanta of energy. The truth is that physics seems more and more to be a study of what Whitehead once called "low-grade organisms." This does not mean that it is identical with the study of living things. The way in which the word organism may be applied at lower physical levels is quite different from that appropriate to living or human experience. Yet it has its analogues.

Two points may be made. First, there is an element of chance or unpredictability running through the physical realm. There is no complete and total determinism, certainly not at the microscopic level. The cosmos might therefore be described as open-ended. At the macroscopic level —big-scale instances—determinism may indeed *seem* to be there, but the activity of the smaller units making up the macrocosm is not absolutely predictable. Second, there is no doubt these days that the ingredients or constituents of the physical order are events or focuses of energy (we may call these "energy events," as I have done earlier). They are not little bits of matter, hard and enduring, bumping against one another. Furthermore, each focus is a concentration of the total cosmic process as it has impinged upon and been used by that particular instance. Thus the interpenetration *within* the energy event is paralleled by interpenetration of that particular energy event *with other* such events. Force, a term much used in physics, is not sheer coercion but the mysterious attraction exercised by one entity, understood as an energy event, upon another. This whole picture is very different from the eighteenth- and nineteenth-century mechanistic scheme.

No responsible scientist today denies that the human species is continuous with the natural order from which it has appeared. It is the cousin of the other primates, yet it is different from the "naked apes," however much it resembles them in certain respects. Sir Julian Huxley has said for many years that there is a distinctive quality about the human species, and contemporary scientific writers are prepared to agree with him. This speciality of the human species has been stated succinctly in Professor Harold K. Schilling's recent book *The New Consciousness in Science and Religion* (Pilgrim Press, 1973, pp. 148-49):

When he [man] arrived, evolutionary activity took on a new character. His extraordinary powers enabled him quickly to bring forth a great variety of utterly new realities: tools and processes, abstractions and symbols, languages and logics, rational analyses and syntheses, measurement and experimentation, and many others equally unprecedented. In this way social rather than biological evolution came to dominate change. The arts and literatures emerged, and the religions, and philosophies, laws, the sciences and technologies—and thus man's cultures and civilizations, with new orders of good and evil, beauty and ugliness, truth and deception. Moreover, there came to this new being the capacity for self-analysis, which was quite unprecedented. He learned to investigate himself, as well as his world, with both critical objectivity and discriminating introspection, and *in depth*. He discovered that his "self," his so-called "nature," and his tremendously varied potentialities are not "possessions" or innate attributes of his own but in large part the gift-consequences of his relationships with other entities and processes and with nature as a whole. Through his knowledge and understanding he has achieved a remarkable degree of self-determination. To a large extent he is now in a position to be both the architect and builder of his own future, which could certainly not be said about any of his evolutionary forebears.

This "whole" view of human existence—I use the adjective whole to indicate an inclusive understanding of human nature—has become increasingly attractive to those working in the many different branches of science that have a bearing on human existence. Process thinking has made its own contribution to this cooperative attempt on the part of physiologists and psychologists, biologists, chemists, anthropologists, and sociologists to see more completely what is distinctively human. By its stress on event and on patterning and integration, by its insistence that relationships constitute an entity, by its concern for an awareness of the depths of human experience (motivations, desires, drives, and "emotional intensity," for example), as well as by its recognition that we are part of the world and continuous with what has gone before us and even now surrounds and affects us, process thought not only has been in agreement with the newer scientific emphasis on "wholeness," but has also contributed a perspective which can give that emphasis a meaningful setting and a context in the structure of things in a dynamic universe.

So it is not surprising that a considerable number of biochemists and zoologists, biophysicists and biologists, psychologists and sociologists, have been attracted to it. One of the world's greatest experts on evolutionary development, the late Dr. Theodosius Dubzshansky (formerly of the famous Rockefeller Institute in New York), has written of its value for his own work. Dr. Joseph Needham and Dr. W.H.

Thorpe, Cambridge authorities on biochemistry and zoology; Dr. A.R. Peacocke, biologist in Cambridge; Professor L.C. Birch, Australian expert on evolutionary changes in the realm of living matter; and Ian Barbour, American physicist, whose special interest has lately been turned toward the ecological problem—these are but a few of the many who have publicly avowed their acceptance of a process way of looking at humankind and the world.

I am not claiming that every worker in every field of science takes such a positive attitude toward process thought. I wish only to indicate that in highly responsible scientific circles this kind of thinking has been valued precisely because of the possibility it offers for a unitary vision of human life, with a serious recognition of what makes our existence distinctive and different from anything else in the natural world but at the same time genuinely part of that natural world.

Whitehead himself was a mathematician, and he was also much interested in and wrote about physics. But he became more and more conscious of the importance of what in North America are called the life sciences, particularly biology and its relationship with physical phenomena. His own major concern in science was to work toward a theory that would relate the sciences having to do with life with those that study nature in its inanimate aspects. Whitehead had concluded that reductionism was impossible because it was absurd to interpret living things through nonliving things. He reversed the procedure and sought to apply the operative principles of life to the realm of energy. He found that this was more rewarding and more illuminating, and capable of greatly enlarging our understanding. Hence his remark, quoted earlier in this chapter, about physics as the investigation of lower-grade organisms and biology as the investigation of higher-grade organisms. But for him this did not entail vitalism. His point was pattern, ordering, arrangement, and increasing harmonization of contrasts, and he believed that there was a remarkable analogy, derived from generalization, running through the whole order of nature.

It is precisely here that the scientists I have mentioned have been most impressed by process thinking, for they also see such an analogy running through the order of nature and they find that the use of that analogy is valuable to them in their work. In his fascinating book *Nature and God* (SCM Press, 1964), Professor Birch has described the ways in which the analogy may be applied in biology. Professor Barbour has done the same for the physical sciences in *Issues in Science and Religion* (SCM Press, 1966). An American medical man, scientist, and philosopher, Prof. Richard H. Overman, has lately written a careful study of the scientific field from this perspective, applying it to the Christian concept of creation. His *Evolution and the Christian Doctrine of Creation* (Westminster Press, 1967) demonstrates the remarkable change that the use of the process conceptuality can make in talk about creation and its mode, and in the scientific corollaries of this world view. These are but three of the recent relatively popular books which in differing ways make some of the points noted above. In the field of psychology, too, it is interesting to note that Professor D.S. Browning of Chicago (especially in his "Psychological and Ontological Perspectives," which appeared in the Chicago *Journal of Religion* in October 1965) surveyed the dynamic and gestalt psychologies, along with the so-called depth psychology of the psychoanalytic school, to show a convergence upon a view of human behavior and human self-awareness that is similar to the organic pattern stressed in process thought. Much the same may be said of work in sociology and anthropology, where today great emphasis is being laid on the structural quality of social life, on the patterns seen in tribal custom, and on the holistic behavior patterns of primitive peoples.

The scientist *as scientist* is not expected to be a philosopher. The scientist has his or her own subject, methodology, and area of competence. That is as it should be. Yet at the same time, the scientist is a person who spends much time with colleagues and is increasingly conscious of the responsibility for use of experimental findings. This consciousness has been especially apparent in the postwar ethical concern shown by experts working in atomic science. The scientist as a person cannot fail to be vitally interested in how scientific work fits into the more general pattern of knowledge and how it is to be employed for good and constructive uses. This is why the scientist needs and desires a vision of things as a whole, in which the scientific speciality has its own place.

My own conversations over many years with my Cambridge colleagues who are dedicated scientists have convinced me that they are seeking almost desperately for a conceptuality that will on the one hand guarantee the validity and autonomy of their own inquiries and on the other hand provide a genuinely humane context for knowledge along with the recognition of responsibility for the results of those inquiries—a responsibility that such a context can provide. When the process conceptuality is expounded to them they are often greatly impressed and in many instances are delighted to embrace it.

This attitude was demonstrated recently after a lecture I was invited to give to the faculty of a large English technological school. My audience was composed of men and women engaged in research or in the application of research to concrete contemporary problems. It was obvious that they could not accept a supernaturalistic view of things, and it was equally obvious that they were dissatisfied with a conception of scientific work which was unrelated to wider issues and insensitive to moral responsibility. My own inadequate summary of the process conceptuality intrigued them, and it was fortunate that there were present some who were well-known as experts in their own fields of study and who therefore could be given as suitable references for further information about the specifically scientific application of the principles I had discussed from the philosophical side. A fascinating evening followed. I believe that this experience is typical of much that is going on today, and this is one of the reasons that in this first part of the present book I seek to give a bird's-eye view of process thought with continual reference to the many different areas of human interest.

In the preceding chapter I tried to say something about another of those areas, the humanities and the arts. It is worth noting that it is often scientists themselves who welcome a discussion of that other area. Lord Snow's portrayal of the "two cultures" is no longer quite accurate. More and more men and women of science are giving marked attention to the humanities and the arts, not only as a relief from concentration on their own disciplines but also as a way of locating those disciplines in a more inclusive setting. As one who is principally concerned with a humanistic discipline, I am also delighted to find that many of my colleagues in that discipline today see clearly the necessity of acquainting themselves with what is going on in the world of science. Process thought has its significance here, too, since one of its main contentions is that a unitary interpretation of existence, human and natural, can make sense of and give sense to all the fields of human inquiry and human enjoyment.

4

Educational Principles

The word education is not derived, as so many think, from the Latin verb *educere*, whose meaning is "educe" or "bring out"; it comes from *educare*, which may be translated as "leading along." Classicists will at once recognize this derivation from the simple fact that the last principal part of the verb *educere* is *eductum*, while that of the verb *educare* is *educatum*; hence, we have "education," not "eduction."

This little academic exercise should help us see that a good deal of talk about education as primarily a "bringing out" of latent knowledge, with consequences for the entire process of instruction, is beside the point. Nobody would wish to deny that such drawing out of possibilities is important, although some would prefer to speak of the enterprise as enabling such possibilities to become actual. But the *first* purpose of education must be the effort to lead young people, and indeed everybody, into a deeper understanding of the historical past and of the concrete world in which they find themselves. Then they may be helped to learn to adapt themselves to the situation which through long development has come to be what and as it is, and seek to prepare for the unexplored and relatively open future ahead of them.

Process thought has much to offer in suggesting a sound perspective on the principles that should govern the work of

—as it should also determine the approach to—education both of the young, whether they be children or adolescents, and of adults who are enrolled in institutions of higher learning or in other ways participate in what appropriately is called the educational process. In this chapter we shall consider some of these principles.

But we may profit from still another brief summary of the relevant affirmations of process thought, about which so much has been said in preceding chapters. First, we live in a world of change, movement, and development, and we ourselves are changing and developing. Second, we live in a world that is societal in quality. Everything is related to, affected by, and itself influences everything else. We belong together, move together, work together, and we find our human fulfillment in the participatory relationships that constitute all entities, from the lowest levels of energy to the highest—even to God, as a later chapter will urge.

Third, the cosmos is kept in order more by lure and persuasion than by the exercise of sheer coercive power. Teilhard de Chardin said that "amorization" is the basic principle in the cosmos, even if force often appears to be more effective. And above all, it is lure, or the invitation to respond, which introduces novelty into a world that is getting somewhere. Thus initial possibilities make their appeal as ways in which realization and fulfillment may be achieved. Fourth, and finally, at every level of creation there is genuine freedom, exercised at the moment when decisions for or against new possibilities must be made. These decisions have their necessary consequences in that the choices made alter the situations that follow them. Furthermore, at the human level such decisions are consciously and responsibly made, although there are obvious restrictions on the degree of freedom present and the chance of the decisions becoming effective.

Dynamism, interrelationship, persuasion or love, and freedom with responsibility in decision are the principles disclosed to us in our own experience and observation, as well as applied by generalization to the rest of the world. In such a creation, in a world like that, with such people as we know ourselves to be, identity is established by the complex unity of *the past*, accepted or rejected; *the present*, in which relationships are enjoyed or refused; and *the future*, whose achievement is to be striven for. These three come together in this or that particular and concrete focus or occasion. Thus I am what I am because my past has been what it has been, because my present relationships are what they are, and because my aim or goal is one I have chosen. When I deal with someone else I must look upon that person as also being just such a focus. But the important point in my existence is not some supposedly isolated or discrete moment in it but the direction or routing that is taken as the past is brought into the present and directed toward the future.

This analysis may be arid and abstract, and it repeats what has been said earlier. Yet the summary may have indicated that the existence it seeks to describe is lively, concrete, and vivid for each of us. I believe that everybody can see that this is so, if and when we use this analysis as a clue to understanding ourselves. We will know ourselves better and hence will be able to know others better too. Nowhere will this knowledge and awareness be more significant than in the way in which we come to look at the total educational process in terms of self and others. All education, at every level, involves a relationship between those who teach and those who learn. No matter how remote the subject matter may seem from personal contacts, a teacher must know his or her pupils, a lecturer the audience, a demonstrator in a laboratory the people with whom work is being done. Very likely, failure by faculty members really to grasp this obvious truth is the occasion for much student discontent today.

Let us now look at some of the implications of process thought for education. I believe there are at least nine implications, and we shall consider them one at a time.

First, it is clear that the educational enterprise, whose purpose is to lead and train students in the understanding of themselves as part of a social development, should promote and foster growth rather than prevent or inhibit it. Sound educational practice will direct itself to helping students change and develop, to become mature. The subject matter required in the curriculum is not meant to stifle initiative. And it is not intended, nor should it seek, to keep students at the level of children who simply repeat by rote what they have been taught to remember.

This is why the responsible educator delights in the students' rejection of old and outworn ideas and rejoices in the acceptance of new ones that promise to bring further personal fulfillment and improve social relationships. A large portion of the old is of course both good and sound and will not be discarded but rather incorporated into newer patterns, learned from experience in the contemporary world, so that the role of the past in the present and toward the future is enhanced and its relative value given proper place. But where things said or done in the past have been disproved, or where they are not useful in new circumstances (save as a matter of historical awareness or of what might be styled archaeological interest), this fact will be acknowledged. There should be respect for the past but no idolatry of it.

Thus, second, education is for life together and for the enhancement of life together. Whatever may be the importance of mere knowledge of facts, past or present—and certainly such knowledge is important—the purpose of the educational enterprise is the development of an openness to truth wherever it may be found. Whitehead once said that the function of reason in human existence is to enhance life, to make life better and to provide opportunities for precisely such an enhancement for as many people as possible. Hence, good education must have as one of its major purposes a participation in the common life at an intelligent level, with due recognition of all that is relevant to augmenting that life.

This common life, however, continues in time. Nobody exists only in the immediately contemporary situation. This truth suggests, in the third place, that an ingredient in education is introduction to the living past which we inherit.

We belong to the total human community, and we do well to enter sympathetically into what has gone before us as well as to know what is going on around us. The past is one of the factors that establishes our human identity—although it is not the only one, since, as we have argued, present and future also have their necessary place as identifying factors. As one of those identifying factors, the past can speak to us with enormous authority, provided it is conveyed by a method of teaching and a kind of study that make what might have been a dead past into a past experienced in the living present. But at the same time, sound education can never forget that students, like their teachers, are actually living *now*. The authority of the past is never absolute, since the issues of the present day, upon which light is thrown by the accumulated experience of the human race, are what each of us must deal with. In the poet's words, "New occasions teach new duties, /Time makes ancient good uncouth."

This is why the future must also be in the picture. Education is not an exercise in "futurology"—that barbarous Latin-Greek hybrid so much used today—but it should be carried on in awareness of the possibilities ahead of us. One of its aims is preparation, especially of the young, for taking part in that future, whatever that part may be. Thus a sound education will be a communication of the wisdom of the past, an introduction to the issues of the present, and a stimulus to intelligent and dedicated action for a better future.

This brings us to our fourth point. What are the contents of good education as far as curriculum goes? My own response is to urge first a broad and humane introduction to the whole human scene, accommodated of course to the capacity of the student to grasp it. Second, there should be an honest and summary communication of the scientific and cultural situation in the present day, with a variety of related material, and dealing with problems and proposed answers. In more advanced education at the university level, there must necessarily be specialization—in one of the sciences, in literature, in philosophy, in the languages, and in much else. But specialization cannot usefully be pursued until there is first a broad base in general education.

Therefore, the fifth point is the communication of information. But that communication must be imaginative, and not by such devices as the memorizing of lists or dates of battles or kings or presidents. When imagination is present, information comes alive. It also comes alive when we recognize that everybody, young or old, is more likely to learn by doing than by accumulating factual details picked up with no real interest on the part of the students. Actual acquaintance means more than meeting the bare facts in a book. To be sure, the basic facts must be acquired, but the *way* in which they are acquired will be different, and the students will find their interests stimulated and quickened when they are invited to have some share in the process of acquisition.

Sixth, factual material must somehow be put to use. This is why good teaching of the sciences always includes a considerable amount of supervised laboratory work in which students are encouraged to make experiments that will enable them to see why a particular statement has become part of the normal stock-in-trade of the scientific world. Chemistry cannot be taught unless the students know about the subject firsthand. Botany is best learned in the field, even though there must be preparation in the classroom or lecture hall. The would-be astronomer needs the experience of personal observation of the heavens. And so it goes, all along the line.

Clearly some academic subjects do not readily lend themselves to this kind of practical work. But all can include personal activity by students: thinking through problems, writing about them, discussing them with teachers and other students. Otherwise, the work of the school will be academic in the bad sense of the word—remote, abstract, dull, tedious, with no likelihood of attracting the students' interest. There may be something to be said for the academic grind as a way of obtaining a minimal collection of important data, but there is nothing to be said for turning the whole educational enterprise into a deadly routine. Indeed, that would not really be education at all but merely a way of satisfying minute examination requirements.

A seventh implication of process thought for education has already been touched on briefly earlier in this chapter. This is the indispensable role of the teacher in the enterprise. Here is where persuasion and attraction have their value. A teacher can and must be firm in direction of the students, but this need not mean teaching by coercive means or trying to force students into unquestioning or unqualified acceptance of thoughts or facts that are remote from their actual existence. Along with the stimulus provided by the invitation to share in a common quest for truth, the central place of what I have called lure can never be forgotten.

Whatever discipline is necessary—and some discipline is required if the whole educational process is not to become anarchic—will be for the sake of the whole group, so that each student will learn to cooperate with others. This is best accomplished by the example of the teacher. Enforced rules dictated from above may seem a convenient shortcut, but observation makes clear that the result will be an overriding of student sensitivity and a smothering of student initiative.

This brings us to the eighth implication. It is difficult to know how to put this into words, but I suggest that it can best be understood as the middle way between old-fashioned subject-centered schooling and ultramodern student-centered schooling. Either of these separately will not do the job. Education in which the subject is so central that the student is forgotten will perhaps work with a very few, but for the great majority it will turn school, college, or university into deadly boredom. That is what a considerable number of university students today feel; it is another element in the so-called student revolt of our time. But when the student is so central that the subject counts for little or nothing, we can arrive at the unfortunate situation that a friend of mine once described as "a confusion of educational process with the pooling of ignorance." In that case, nothing is really learned. The young daughter of an acquaintance of mine spoke to the point when she told me that at her school there were no requirements of any kind and that, as a result, she "got bored stiff with having to do every day what she wanted to do." In fact, all students and especially young people deeply appreciate and value academic discipline if by discipline we mean both the subject-matter to be studied and some set requirements in the mastering of it.

The ninth and last implication is in many ways the most important of all since it sums up a good deal of what has been said earlier. This implication is derived from one of the most valuable insights of process thought, namely, that each of us is not only an intellect, not only a rational being with some capacity to learn truth, not only a will to be taught to strive and struggle—human beings are supremely sensitive, desiring, feeling, appreciating, and valuing beings. A grave defect in much conventional education is that it tends to forget this truth. I have spoken of dullness and boredom in the intellectual area; I must now add that ugliness, or its companions prettiness and vulgarity, are equally dangerous if we hope to assist people in coming to their best fulfillment in a life of intense satisfaction. I said as much in the earlier chapter on the humanities.

In whatever way we find possible, innate aesthetic sensitivity, not least in the young person, needs to be stimulated, cultivated, and enhanced. One is often astounded to see how quite young children will respond to beauty of word and sound and sight, of color and music. An education that misses out on these will be inadequate to the wholeness of human existence, even if it may seem to accomplish its supposedly primary intellectual objective.

I am convinced that when these implications are remembered, when education reckons with them, the results will far exceed our expectations. The details of their application need to be worked out, of course; one of the tasks of theorists and practitioners in education is to do just this. But when they are worked out, education will become more attractive and compelling to those who hitherto have so often regarded themselves as only its victims. They will be no longer victims but genuine participants in the enterprise. And that will be all to the good.

What has been said here about education and especially our insistence on the importance of the aesthetic in its broadest sense—feelings, desires, appreciation, valuation, and response to the lovely or beautiful in its many manifestations—is highly relevant to the subject of our next chapters, which have to do with the moral and religious aspect of life as illuminated by process thought. There has been a tendency in Christian circles, above all in those of Protestant allegiance, to emphasize the ethical side of religion. I do not wish to minimize that side, and in the next chapter I shall consider the ethical question and its significance as process thought throws light on it. But religion is largely a matter of deeply felt relationships, of response to beauty (God was once said to be "the altogether lovely"), of appreciation, and of a sense of value. This is not to imply that it is merely fanciful, but it does tell us that religion is very much a matter of profound imagination.

So when we look at the religious aspect of human existence and see what contributions process thought may have to make to this inescapable and indestructible manifestation of the human spirit, we shall need to emphasize that it is to be understood not in the wooden fashion that so often has prevailed in institutional churches and in conventional religious communities but as a matter of imaginative and aesthetic response to the human situation and to whatever is supremely worshipful in the cosmos—that is, to what religion calls "God."

5

Moral Implications

Not long ago, a "Humanist Manifesto" was published and signed by more than a hundred leaders in various fields coming from English-speaking countries around the world. The signatories declared their conviction that "no God will save us; we must save ourselves" as we face the problems for which humanity must find a solution if human existence is to continue on this planet. Much of the manifesto was directed against "God" although it was addressed to a specific *concept* of God—and about this we shall speak in Chapter 7. But there was one statement that is of special interest to us as in our consideration of the moral implications of process thought. "We affirm that moral values derive their source from human experience," the humanist statement ran. "Ethics is autonomous and situational, needing no theological or ideological sanction." And the manifesto denounced any morality that is supposed to be founded on "promises of immortal salvation or fear of eternal damnation."

In all this we have a frank and total rejection of an ethic whose source and validation is in some power or person entirely external to humankind. The popular notion that moral behavior is possible only when it is backed by a calculus of divinely granted rewards and punishments was refuted. If there is to be any sound ethic, we were told by the people who issued the manifesto, it must be derived from human experience, related to the situations in which people find themselves, and given what was called "autonomy"—by which was meant a denial of a standard imposed from outside, or apart from, the human experience with which we are all familiar.

When we consider the enormous amount of suffering that various traditional ethical systems have inflicted on men, women, and children, we may well sympathize with the attitude of the signers of that manifesto. Human societies, both civil and ecclesiastical, have been responsible for appalling damage to human personality in requiring obedience to rules or codes that violate freedom by putting people into moral straitjackets and by trying to make people good by legal sanctions. But we may well ask if it is really possible to have an ethic that is entirely autonomous and that is derived solely from human experience, for while supranaturalistic sanctions, and promises of reward or fear of punishment, can never produce genuine goodness, the general sense of humankind has been plain enough: that in some fashion or other goodness is in accordance with the structure of things, in some relationship with the grain of the universe, or what Whitehead once called the "rightness" that runs through everything.

The question frequently being asked in our day is whether there are *any* moral absolutes or whether *everything* is relative. Many would say that absolutes are not for finite humanity to know; but many would say that if everything is relative, then there can be no morality at all. The Humanist Manifesto itself appeals to sympathy, compassion, and understanding as being in some undefined fashion absolute in nature. It does not commend an ethic of dog eat dog, nor does it urge that each person should be for himself or herself, and the devil take the hindmost. On the contrary, it asks for cooperation, social awareness and concern, and above all a chance for men and women to realize fully their potential personhood. These are taken as having what may properly be styled a permanent character, although they are not given that character because some deus ex machina has established them.

We have seen that process thought is particularly insistent upon human existence as organic to the world of nature, so that an awareness of that existence is important for our grasp of what the world is like. Human life emerged from the wider cosmic order, it belongs to it, and it depends on it. Hence, it is not unreasonable to conclude that human existence discloses something about it. We have also seen another emphasis in the process perspective: that human experience takes persuasion to be better than force, and that somehow the history of the human race's development is in fact the story of the victory of persuasion over force. Might it not then be the case that human experience *in this deeper sense*, with its conviction about the centrality of persuasion (call it love, if you wish), does indeed provide a grounding for morality? Since men and women live one with another in common human situations, in an interrelationship through common sharing in their existence, might it not be the case that a consideration of the meaning of this common life will give us some clue to an ethic that will certainly be autonomous yet be most profoundly associated with the cosmic structure and the cosmic dynamic?

This is a sound way of reasoning. While there is plenty of evil in the natural order, and a great deal of evil in humankind's selfish willing and acting, the insight of the ages (in all developing cultures and as people deepen their sensitivity) tells us that despite the evil, and even in conflict with it, there is a movement toward sharing, toward participation, toward community, toward love. It is not absurd to put this in the language of Teilhard de Chardin, the French paleontologist, and speak of "amorization"—a development in love and in loving—as the one thing upon which we may rely and in which we may put our ultimate trust.

If we accept such a view, there is surely *one* absolute amidst all the relativities of human experience. That absolute is nothing other than love itself, with its corollary in the imperative that we should live in, grow in, express, and share love. This is the starting point for our consideration of the moral implications of process thought. But it does not stand alone, for there is the dynamic or "becoming" aspect of human existence, as men and women either move toward or move away from the fulfillment or actualization of their potentialities. When we bring together the imperative of love and the fact of human "becoming," and also remember that we are social creatures who necessarily live in community with our human brothers and sisters, the fundamental ethical question becomes plain: Am I, are you, moving in the direction of deeper and more inclusive love of our neighbors, or am I, are you, moving in the opposite direction?

Love in this sense can then be taken as absolute, with its associated imperative to loving relationships. Everything else can be regarded as relative, including conventional moral codes, rules, and regulations, however much the latter may have been thought to be divinely revealed, as many have described the Ten Commandments, or to be divinely implanted in the human nature we share, like the "natural law" about which traditional ethical theory has often spoken. This ordering of priorities with love as supreme and laws as secondary is no new invention. Jesus enunciated it in saying that love of God and of our neighbors "sums up" or "fulfills" the older Jewish law. Paul said the same: love is the fulfilling of the law. Gautama Buddha taught it, although with a more passive emphasis in his way of phrasing it. Confucius and Lao-Tze in China accepted a similar ethic. The classical Christian theological tradition has explicitly recognized this ordering, as when, for example, Thomas Aquinas said that the *nova lex*, "the new law" that he spoke of as being "in our hearts," is the "charity" that comprehends all the other virtues.

The discussion between humanists of goodwill (like the signers of the Humanist Manifesto) and those of us who wish to urge some cosmic grounding for moral values has been bedeviled by the way in which so much of our inherited ethical teaching has invoked sanctions that are not really moral at all but essentially external impositions whose result is to turn people into robots. Yet religious people at their best have seen more deeply than that. They have glimpsed but not always been able to state properly the point I made above, namely, that there is in the cosmos a movement toward moral goodness, summed up in love and in action-in-love, which seeks for human cooperation and human expression. Conversely, we may well believe that the humanist urge for sharing in the common life as the only viable basis for true fulfillment of human potentiality is itself a reflection of and an instrument for a greater love among humans because of a cosmic sharing together. What matters most of all, then, is awareness of the absolute nature of love, sharing, participation, and commonality. At this point both the humanist and the religious man or woman can come together in concrete and practical ways.

According to the process way of thinking, love is indeed the absolute. This is because the purpose of creation is the development of possibilities in relationship at every level—in a dim and inarticulate fashion below the human and in more fully conscious fashion as we rise in the creative process to the human level where we find ourselves. This is not to imply that there need be no guidelines or intimations about how love may best be put to work. We need not throw away the moral heritage that has come to us through the centuries, but neither need we give its dictates absolute status. We can learn from our ancestors, and if process thinking is right, we *must* do this since the past has provided us with the materials in terms of which present decisions may be made, and has also made us what we now are. Our moral slant, our recognition of the centrality of love, and our concern for sharing are part of that inheritance. But to learn from the past does not mean that one must be tied to it. In many areas we have new knowledge that may seriously modify earlier positions, and this new knowledge cannot be dismissed out of hand.

I mention two examples of necessary moral change among the many that might be cited. Consider how what we have learned about human sexuality, with respect both to its origins and to its sociological aspects, has altered the general attitude toward sexual desire and expression. The next chapter will discuss this in detail. Or consider how our recent experience has brought home to us vividly the imperatives of ecological responsibility. No longer can we regard ourselves as rulers of the whole earth, with no concern for the consequences of what we do with natural resources, the environment, and the relationship that exists between the human and the natural.

We urgently need also to attend to the difference that is made in moral judgment once we take seriously the developmental or "becoming" nature of human existence. In a day when it was assumed that this existence was a finished product, "an individual substance of a rational nature" created much as it now is, judgment could be given with respect to this or that specific act which was or was not "according to human nature." But when we see that each of us is a self-conscious "routing" in which the past is used as an occasion for decisions in the present and toward goals that lure us from a nondeterminated future, moral judgment must be in terms of precisely that routing or direction. Am I *"becoming"* more fully an actualized human being? Am I deciding to use my potentialities in the most fruitful manner? Am I on my way to realizing myself as a lover in company with my neighbors? Am I making decisions or choices, am I acting or speaking, so that more widely shared good is established? In other words, the moral question for each of us has to do with where we are going, how we are getting there, and the way in which our own particular routing is contributing to the wider social good—a social good that is part of the cosmic movement toward amorization.

Of course, this means that the situational aspect of ethical issues, to which the Humanist Manifesto quite rightly made reference, must be seen as of the greatest importance. We exist with our neighbors in *particular* conditions and under *particular* circumstances, not in moral abstraction. Moral judgments therefore cannot be made abstractly, as if each person might be looked at in isolation. On the contrary, the

57

old sayings which tell us that circumstances alter cases and that context largely determines content have to be taken seriously. Where I am, with whom I live, my past life, where I may be going—everything that has gone to make me up and everything that now affects me—all this must be taken into account just as much as the somewhat artificial question "Who am I?" asked (as so often it has been) in abstraction from everything else.

A presupposition basic to all ethical discussion is freedom of choice. This need not be complete freedom; in any event, complete freedom does not exist. But the process position maintains, and has gone a long way toward demonstrating, that there is indeed a genuine freedom running straight through the world. At the human level, of course, that freedom is distinctive in its being consciously and responsibly exercised. I find it difficult to see how Buckminster Fuller, one of the signers of the Manifesto, could join with his co-signers in a call for ethical decision when he has published extensively with the aim of showing that there *is* no freedom to decide. Perhaps one might apply to him and to others like him Whitehead's comment that people whose purpose is to show that there is no purpose constitute an interesting subject for study! Plainly they do have a purpose. Plainly they are appealing to others to decide freely that what they are proposing is valid and right. Freedom is so much an assumption of all human effort that only a very clever person would waste time trying to show that it does not exist!

In what sense can one speak of a self that is both free and responsible? The problem of human identity has always been a difficult one. There have been almost as many definitions on the subject as there have been writers. But the conventional definition has perhaps been that identity is established by a soul or mind or spirit introduced into, but separable from, the body in which it dwells. This position has been taken by most traditional Christian theologians; its influence has pervaded Western culture. In the Far East, however, there has been a long tradition, chiefly among Buddhists, that there is no identifiable soul in addition to the body but rather a series of experiences held in some sort of genuine and experienced unity by memory and by the necessity (in the present) of making decisions toward future goals. That view resembles the process way of seeing the matter. A process conceptuality cannot talk of a soul in the conventional sense, since it sees every entity or event in the world as essentially a unity with one pole in the material world of hard fact and the other in the realm of possible fulfillment. At the human level, there is a conscious capacity to envision the realizing of new possibility. In other words, process thought is through and through psychosomatic with respect to human existence. Each of us is a complex patterning of the physical and the mental, just as each of us is both *this* self, as being *this* particular "routing," and also a specific instance of a wider social belonging.

So we might say that human identity is established by the three tenses: by the *past*, which is remembered and used; by the *present*, in which decisions are made; and by the *future* aim of fulfillment, through the achievement of goals either positively or negatively. Thus, I am who and what I am because of the past that is distinctively mine and nobody else's, because of the present influences I feel and the present decisions I make, and because of the purpose I have before me, however vaguely I may perceive it. At the human level, this identity has the added quality of self-awareness or self-consciousness. Somewhere and somehow in the evolutionary process there emerged a specifically human kind of routing —a series of successive moments of experience—whose characteristic quality is the capacity to *know* that routing and to grasp what is going on in it.

Primarily, this selfhood is given in human memory, both conscious and subconscious and also visceral. Human memory is peculiar in that it makes possible the kind of introspective knowledge that enables me to speak of *my* routing as "myself" and to distinguish that self from other selves which are each in a similar case. But this must not be pushed too far, since there is also a sense in which I can have a conscious awareness and something like an introspective knowledge of other selves too. This sympathetic identification with others, so that I live in them and they in me, is given in varying degrees of intimacy. Such identification reaches its fullest expression when I am "in love" with another and by my loving understanding can get aboard the other's life or at least share to a considerable degree with the other in his or her series of experiences.

Such continuity of experiences, which make me a self because I am aware of them but also make me a self with others because I can enter into their ongoing movement, is the basis for responsibility. In specific instances, I assume the obligations that follow from my decisions and their results. But in another way I am also being created anew with each succeeding experience, so that judgment must always be in terms of directions taken rather than in terms of supposedly isolated moments that stand by themselves. This perspective gives us hope for change and the expectation that novelty may occur in any self's continuing experience. That is why judgment should always be tempered by mercy; there is always the chance that change for the better (that is, for a decision toward a fulfillment shared with others) will take place.

An ethic built upon the process conceptuality will be very different from a static and legalistic law ethic; it will be personalized and socialized. By *personalized* I mean that it will be relevant to the person or self, in that person's concrete situation, where and how and as that person is. By *socialized* I mean that it will see that the person does not and cannot exist in separation from other persons or from the society of which both are part.

There is here an interesting convergence of the existentialist analysis of what it feels like to be human, and the world view with respect to the whole cosmos enunciated in process thought. Teilhard de Chardin once suggested, although in a quite different context, that the former can provide the "inside," the latter the "outside," of our understanding of the total human condition in the world. We can put it another way and say that the existentialist description of human existence in its deepest self-awareness has to do with what Whitehead called "emotional intensity," while the process view gives a description of the "energetic activity" that characterizes the world as we observe it. The two fit together in giving us a comprehensive picture.

In sum, each human life is a body-mind complex in which both material and mental aspects have their part to play. Each of us is a person or self because we are consciously aware of the continuity of the experiences that take place along our specific routing. Each is free to make relevant decisions that are limited in scope but that nevertheless largely determine how things will go in the future. Each is responsible for such decisions because each is thus aware of what is going on and what is being done about that going on. And the criterion by which we may judge the rightness of decisions with their consequent actions is love, which is sharing, mutuality, giving-and-receiving, openness, sympathy, self-identification, concern for the good of others, and readiness even to suffer for that shared good.

How this will work itself out in social, economic, political, racial, and other areas of human experience is dependent upon the goodwill of men and women. It is also dependent upon the intelligence they apply to the problems they must face. But justice is not alien to love; it is the way in which love works and is effective in circumstances that include large numbers of people—classes, races, nations, parties. The adaptation of love to varying situations will be different in this place and that, in this age and that, for this need and with this demand. Workability is one of the tests here. Yet all the time, the one "absolute" to which appeal can be made and which will provide the necessary motivation for action is *love*—not sentimentality or superficial emotion, of course, but genuine love in the sense noted above.

Process thought would say that when human decisions and human actions are responsive to such love, they are right. It would claim that they are then cosmically grounded and validated. We can put this in specifically Christian moral-religious language. Since God *is* love, human loving is the only possible interpretation of, meaning in, and imperative for genuinely moral life. To state it in that way makes clear that each man and woman is constantly challenged to be a cocreator of good, and a co-worker in good, with the cosmic thrust toward good that religious people name God, thus participating in the enormously demanding effort to overcome evil, injustice, oppression, suffering, and whatever else in the creation works against that good.

6

Human Sexuality

"It is in the controversial field of sexuality that the process theologians have made their real contribution to ethical thought today." So said the author of a book published in Britain a few years ago. He believes that sexuality is "one area where, because of the profound element of 'mystery' in inter-personal relationships, the secular kind of pragmatism has little to offer" (A.G. Woollard, *Progress: A Christian Doctrine?*, SPCK, 1972). A process approach certainly has the possibility of making a significant contribution to this "mysterious" area.

My purpose in the present chapter is to make some suggestions about this from the side of Christian faith and Christian morality, interpreted in terms of process thought. Because these are merely suggestions, others who are more expert in the field of ethical theory may be led to consider the matter in greater detail. My only excuse for writing on the subject is that it seems important to include it in a book on process thought and its use. Furthermore, as a personal apology, I am a human being and hence a sexual creature; and I am a Christian in faith, however imperfect that faith may be. As such, and as an adherent of the process conceptuality, I believe one can show how all three of these can fit together in a discussion of human sexuality.

One of the difficulties in much that has been written or said about human sexuality is that it has been altogether too much based upon what Mr. Woollard calls a "secular kind of pragmatism." That is to say, it is not grounded in a total view of human nature. When it talks about "man," in the generic sense, it looks at human life and speaks about it with no regard for what I have styled the cosmic context, the wider perspective of the world's creative dynamic and structure. In addition, it is often prepared to consider human sexuality as an aspect or element in human beings that are assumed to exist as fixed entities—as if one could speak of static and changeless "human nature." Hence, I begin with a brief statement about human existence in its cosmic setting when seen from a process perspective and interpreted in the light of Christian faith.

We have said repeatedly that humans exist in a world which is marked by movement and change and where the basic constituents are not things but events or occurrences. All such energy events mutually affect and influence one another; "reality is a *social* process," to use the words of Charles Hartshorne. Any energy event, and any grouping or society of such events, builds upon the inherited past, in relationship with which it makes its decisions in the present. And it has a future reference, since the potentialities given in its emerging provide it with an initial aim to which it may so respond that this initial aim becomes the event's own subjective aim. Furthermore, there is freedom to choose or decide whether this shall or shall not take place. Such a freedom runs through the whole cosmos at every level and with the appropriate variations in subjective awareness of its existence. Thus the world is not predetermined but is in many ways an open world, although of course there are sufficient continuities or regularities to maintain it as a cosmos and to prevent disintegration into anarchic chaos. This creation neither explains itself nor finds its meaning in itself; there is a reality that is the source of potentiality and the recipient of achievement, a reality that works in the created order to provide aims, to lure events toward actualizing such aims, and then to accept into itself the good that this actualization accomplished. This source and recipient we call *God*, whose character and whose manner of working are nothing other than Love-in-act. We have argued for this "vision of reality" in earlier chapters, and we shall return to it in the next chapter. Here, however, we must add that for Christian faith the source and recipient which is Love-in-act is believed to be expressed decisively and specifically, yet not exclusively and without parallel, in the event we name when we say *Jesus Christ*. To use Schubert Ogden's word, Jesus Christ is taken to *re-present* what God is always and everywhere up to, what God is always and everywhere doing, and what God is always and everywhere seeking to achieve in the world—with which God is unfailingly related and with which God is in a relationship of mutual influence.

It is against such a background that a Christian process thinker sees human existence. Somewhere along the evolutionary line specifically human existence emerged, marked by a notable degree of awareness and self-awareness, able to appreciate and value, capable of response to possibilities, and accountable for choices made and for their consequences. What then does it mean to be human? I suggest that it means to be *on the way to becoming human*, that is, on the way toward actualizing human potentialities and in so doing becoming more open to the possibility of reflecting the Love that is God and of serving as the personalized and personalizing agent for that Love. To be human is to be moving toward the image of God, who *is* Love, to be moving also toward a richer existence as created, finite, and inevitably defective lovers.

However, because we are not souls who have bodies but animated bodies with mental and spiritual capacity, the business of becoming a lover includes our embodied, psychosomatic, and socially conditioned nature. This tells us that our human development in loving has for its basis the fact of our being physiologically and psychologically sexual creatures. If angels exist and are "disembodied intelligences" (as defined by Thomas Aquinas), we do not know how they learn to love. But for us humans, who are bodies quite as much as minds and spirits, such growth must be by those bodies as well as by activity of a mental or spiritual kind. We may notice that at the animal level sexuality is the means by which a species is continued through reproduction, while at the human level sexuality has become the basis for unitive or conjunctive relationships. Reproduction is indeed appropriate and probable in those relationships where it can occur, but for specifically human existence procreation should be conscientiously and responsibly undertaken, not reduced entirely to the biological consequence of the genital union of male and female bodies.

In these paragraphs I have tried to give the presuppositions we should have in mind when we speak of human sexuality. But perhaps I have not sufficiently stressed still another important matter, namely, that in all human decisions, and the actions that are consequent upon them, there is likely to be serious distortion of, or a sadly imperfect response to, the possibilities for good. Indeed, such distortion and imperfection is well nigh inevitable. There is an accumulation of social wrongdoing which influences us; there is the easy availability of less adequate satisfaction of desire. This means that human existence is unhappily marked by estrangement from God or Love-in-act and by alienation from the true development of selfhood. Religion calls this estrangement and alienation "sin." What is more, in no area of human experience is it so easy to deny or violate Love-in-act and to remain content in superficial and unfulfilling decisions and actions as it is in the realm of sexual behavior. Centuries ago Augustine saw this clearly enough, although he discussed it in a fashion that now seems jaundiced and cynical. Suffice it to say that it is precisely because sexuality is so central to humans as lovers-in-the-making that its misuse or distortion is a frightening, because readily observable, aspect of our existence. Yet there is no area where splendid opportunities for genuine fulfillment and joy may more wonderfully be found. Hence there is an ambiguity in human sexuality that may stand as a symbol for the ambiguity of all human life in its genuine potentiality and in its tragic failure.

Sexuality is a good thing in itself, and so are sexual acts in themselves. I am making an important distinction here. By *sexuality* I mean the all-pervasive erotic aspect of human existence that is present in all we say and think and do, in every relationship with others and also in our relationship with God as the source of human "refreshment and companionship." By *sexual acts* or *sex* I mean explicitly genital behavior in which human physiological sexual contact, with its psychological and emotional concomitants, is the means for a unitive or conjunctive relationship. Sexual acts, or sex, express the wider "sexuality"; they are enormously satisfying and they can establish deep and intimate one-to-one relationships with others.

There are three types of sexual activity in which human beings may act upon and express their wider sexuality: heterosexual, homosexual, and celibate. The last named may surprise some readers, but for reasons given later I am convinced that it should be included.

The heterosexual mode of expression is obviously the most common. Boy meets girl, boy loves girl, boy marries girl— so it has gone in human history. Society has recognized this by setting up a pattern of relationship which in our Western culture is predominantly monogamous and finds its chief manifestation in matrimony, although there have been and are other cultures that have taken a different line in their attitude toward heterosexuality. So usual is the heterosexual expression, so much is it the common mode, that our Western ethical tradition has spoken of it as normal. I am not suggesting that homosexuality and celibacy are abnormal or unnatural, and I shall discuss the matter later. Nonetheless, nobody can doubt that most people have found, and still find, heterosexual genital contact, enjoyed within some societal context, satisfactory for them and their preferred way of intimate relationship with others of the human race.

There may be considerable diversity in heterosexual relationships, and there is today dissatisfaction with the inherited pattern. But it is not my purpose here to go into this, or to consider the various modern patterns, the question of divorce after marriage, the case often made for group marriages, and the like. Generally speaking, we find everywhere wide acceptance of heterosexuality where marriage is the aim and where the procreation of children is welcomed. We find that there is usually a wish to bring into existence a family as a cell of shared love, in which all members participate in mutuality or giving-and-receiving. At its best, this is a lovely and ennobling thing. Heterosexual marriage may well be preceded by some degree of experimentation and experience, but for the most part the aim is for boy to marry girl and girl to marry boy. Christian moral thinking has accepted this and has given marriage a special blessing, surrounding it with the aura of divine approval even if it has not always realistically grasped the fact that marriage is not inevitably an ideal state and that to insist on its continuance when love is absent is to condone what in effect is legalized rape and hence hardly an appropriate symbol for the Christian idea of marriage as representing "the mystical union of Christ and his Church."

Second, there is homosexuality. Many believe it is wrong to regard this as a legitimate mode of genital sexual contact; they condemn it as unnatural and deviant. I cannot agree. I hold that the approximately 10 percent of the world population who are homosexual in inclination and whose only satisfying sexual expression is that with someone of their own gender are acting in a fashion which is entirely normal and natural for them. It is natural and normal for people with that kind of sexual attraction and desire to wish to behave homosexually. Thus they are not deviant, although they are different from the vast majority of the human race.

In our Western tradition, biblical texts, taken literally or fundamentalistically, have been used to condemn all homosexual acts, and a particular version of natural moral law has also relegated homosexuals to the category of freaks. But if we interpret such texts in their appropriate context and with due regard for their cultural setting, and if we regard the argument from natural law as lacking *content* (even if Aquinas' generalized summary of that law as "doing good, not evil" is *formally* true), we must acknowledge the goodness of homosexuality when and as it is practiced with due regard for the genuine moral norms, to which I shall refer at the end of this chapter.

The historical record of the Christian churches and of human society generally with respect to homosexuals is appalling. Men and women have been condemned, rejected, and led to think of themselves as the worst of sinners, whereas they ought to have been welcomed, accepted, and treated as human beings exactly like their heterosexual brothers and sisters, the one difference being the direction of their sexual drive. In due course, surely a more humane, more Christian, and more loving and understanding attitude will prevail, not least because society at large is slowly but certainly coming to accept this position about homosexuals.

Finally, there is the celibate expression of human sexuality. This is not an explicitly genital mode of contact, but it *is* a way of sexual living that makes its appeal to those who by religious vocation (e.g., monks and nuns) or a call to a particular kind of human service (e.g., Dag Hammarskjöld) or some necessity (e.g., those who cannot find a life partner or a homosexual comradeship available) are forced to live without a genital way of being sexual. Of course, the danger here is that such persons may repress their sexuality, but this need not be the case. Many of us can think of monks and nuns (as well as of others who are not vocationally celibate but nonetheless actually so) who have been enabled to live fully and healthily, rechanneling their sexual drive toward other modes of expression that can make them loving, concerned, caring, and deeply devoted and committed people.

I have omitted autoerotic sexual activity from my list, not because it is evil in itself—today there is general agreement that this is not the case—but because it fails to include the social reference which is integral to human existence as such, as I held in discussing human nature. Youthful and adolescent masturbation certainly is not wicked; in older persons it will very likely be harmless, in the absence of other kinds of sexual activity and as a means of relieving physical sexual tension. However, it is almost always *faute de mieux*. The reason for this is that it is usual, even natural (to use here the question-begging adjective), for human sexual expression to be *with others* precisely because (as I have argued) human existence is a social existence, where sociality is the correlative of personality.

Let us now turn to what elsewhere I have styled the "controls" for the concrete actual sexual expression of pervasive human sexuality (see my book *Love and Control in Sexuality*, United Church Press, 1974). Perhaps guidelines would have been a better term, and in what follows I shall use it.

It seems that in all expressions of human sexuality, including especially the explicitly genital ones, there are five such guidelines: (1) Always act with due regard for the other as more than merely a means for self-gratification. (2) Always treat the other as a person, not as a thing. (3) Always act with responsibility for the other's fulfillment and human growth; hence, aim at as much permanence as is possible for the relationship. (4) Always act with responsibility for the other's self-esteem and with due consideration for the consequences of one's actions. (5) Always act in such a fashion that the act is seen in its wider and more inclusive context. The basic intention in all five guidelines is to make possible the expression of love, both given and received. By love I mean, as I have already stressed, a relationship of sharing, mutuality, openness, self-giving, and gracious receiving, which is very different from sentimentality or emotionalism or easy toleration. Indeed, love has few more dangerous enemies than those last three, exactly because they give a specious appearance of *being* love, whereas they are denials of its true nature or cheap evasions of its claims upon us.

First, then, it is a violation of love to use another person for one's own gratification, without regard for that other's wishes or feelings. The reason is plain enough, since it is characteristic of love to seek a mutual relationship in which the welfare of the other is given first place. Second, it is a violation of love to treat somebody else as an object or thing, to be manipulated as one likes, rather than as a person with whom one is always concerned *as* a person. The reason is that love always personalizes and regards the other as "thou," or at the very least as "you." Third, it is a violation of love to seek to hurt or damage—at worst to wish to destroy—another or to "possess" the other for a time, with no concern for continuation of relationship. The reason is that love is always concerned to help, heal, and build up, never to harm another, and delights in establishing an enduring association. Fourth, it is a violation of love to disregard another, to imperil another's self-esteem, to reject one's own accountability for another, and to fail to consider the consequences of what one has done to and with another. The reason is that love is always respectful, always responsive to others, always prepared to take upon itself the consequences that may follow from actions undertaken with them. Fifth, it is a violation of love to center one's whole attention upon and confine one's interest to the strictly physical, without concern for wider personal context and social implications. The reason is that love is always proportionate in its concern and tries to see another as a whole human being in a whole human context.

This discussion of guidelines is very brief, to be sure, but I trust that it suggests a viable code for sexual behavior. Note that they are applicable both to wider human sexuality and to explicit physical sex. That is as it should be, since the point of explicit sexual acts is that they are the chief way or ways, among other ways, in which the human erotic drive toward union or conjunction manifests itself.

Some may wish for more precise and detailed regulations for sexual behavior in the narrower sense, but I believe that in this area of human experience, perhaps above all others, room must be left for spontaneity and freshness. Also, we need to recognize that we are living in a period of enormous change in the understanding of human sexuality and human sex. Out of this will come most certainly a new set of values and a new direction for conduct which will commend themselves as both human and humane. And if we have the courage to bring Christian faith into the picture, that new understanding may be more deeply Christian both in outlook and judgment. I am no prophet, and I cannot say in detail what this new set of values and new direction for conduct will be like. But I believe it was hinted at in the words of a young Cambridge undergraduate who told me that what he and most of his friends aimed at in their sexual behavior were three things: *permissiveness,* within the range of social decency and acceptance; *affection,* by which he meant genuine caring and the beginning of real love; and *responsibility,* which he defined as readiness to stand up and take the consequences for any and every sort of human contact.

I must make one final comment, which has to do with the religious dimension of human sexuality in all its aspects. I believe that the Christian churches, especially the more conservative ones, have been inclined to make both too much and too little of explicit physical sexual behavior. They have made too much of it in that they have assumed that if it differs from the conventional pattern of heterosexuality it must be wrong, more particularly if it includes approximations to or actual engagement in coition. And they have assumed that a single sexual episode will determine the whole direction of human lives. But the churches have also made too little of explicit sexual behavior because they have failed to see that here is one of the basic vitalities of human existence and therefore an important clue to the deepest drive in the cosmos toward what Teilhard de Chardin called "amorization." In other words, they have failed to relate human sexuality, in its genital expression, to process and sociality, which is the way God works in the world.

An example of this double error is the feeling that many Christians have been led to entertain about sex and worship. For many years the Catholic Christian has thought it improper to come to the holy table for communion shortly after engaging in sexual relations. Let me relate what I said to two people in their early twenties who told me that they liked to receive communion together after they had made love the night before. They were deeply in love and had lived together for some years. They were devout Christians. I told them, "Speaking humanly, as I must since I am not God, I am sure that God is delighted to unite you in the divine love after you have been united in your human love." God is happy when people enjoy good sex and rejoices enormously when they truly "make love."

There is a poem by Richard Hovey, included in his collection *More Songs from Vagabondia*, which speaks of the joy experienced in some moments of human life, one of which is the delight and thrill of making love, surely one of the highest experiences any man or woman can know. In his poem Hovey says that such human joy is forever part of the *divine* joy, received and remembered in the life of God:

> God has said, "Ye shall fail and perish,
> But the thrill you have felt tonight
> I shall keep in my heart and cherish
> When the worlds have passed into night."

That is good process thinking. It is also profoundly relevant to the process insistence that nothing valuable achieved and known in the experience of human beings is ever lost. Such an insistence opens the way for our next chapter on religion as interpreted in process thought.

7

The Religious
Understanding

In the introductory chapter we spoke of the "secular" spirit of our age, with its insistence upon the recognition of human capacity and human responsibility and with its refusal to look to a *deus ex machina* who will intervene in the world to set things right when they go wrong and upon whose shoulders blame for that wrong can always be placed. But we also pointed out that the "religious" spirit is by no means absent today, although frequently it expresses itself in ways very different from older and more conventional religious attitudes and practices.

Many of us believe that the process conceptuality can make a significant and indeed invaluable contribution to the religious aspect of human existence. There are two reasons for this. First, since process thought concerns itself with the totality of human experience, it must necessarily take very seriously the fact of the religious vision and the claim of countless millions of people of every race and nation and age to have enjoyed some kind of contact with a reality greater than humankind or nature, through which refreshment and companionship have been given. Second, a consistent acceptance of process generalizations about how things go in the world can provide the material for the radical reconception, of what can be affirmed about that reality greater than humankind or nature—about *God,* to use the traditional word for that reality. Certainly, new ways of speaking about God are needed today.

Since my readers are, like me, heirs of Western culture, I shall limit our discussion of religion to the ways in which that culture has usually portrayed the divine, and then attempt a process reconception of the situation. Others, more competent than I, could doubtless do the same for Eastern culture, whether it be Indian or Chinese or some other type. In our Western culture, which for at least nineteen hundred years has been profoundly affected by Christian thinking, great theologians have developed a conception of deity that most people probably regard as the one and only possible view. This conception was worked out in the first three centuries of the Christian era, given more precise shape in the Middle Ages, and has been more or less accommodated to the newer knowledge of modern times in recent years. With Professor Charles Hartshorne, we may call this conception of deity "classical theism." What does it include?

Primarily, it asserts that God is first mover or first cause of everything else. To say "first," of course, is not necessarily to speak in temporal terms; essentially it is to assert *logical* priority. However creation was accomplished, it is all the work of a deity who is the ultimate and finally responsible causative agent; secondary causation, such as we know in our own experience of the world, is derivative from and in every respect dependent upon the first cause. In a great deal of Western thought this has entailed a sort of omni-voluntarism, a belief that it is God's will alone that is effective in the world. Human or creaturely acts do not modify or influence the working of that divine will but can only serve as its agents. Hence God is omnipotent. *All* power is really God's. Whatever appearance of power is exercised elsewhere or otherwise can never deflect or affect the divine. Thus God is almighty in the obvious sense of being able to do *anything*—or so the simpleminded have been led to think. More sophisticated theologians have qualified this outrageous notion by saying that God can do nothing which is irrational, such as make square circles, or which is contrary to God's own nature and purpose, which are assumed to be good in some ultimate sense, and therefore that God cannot engage in genuinely evil acts. But, there is of course a great deal of evil in the world, and if God is indeed omnipotent, omni-competent, and omni-voluntarist, somehow God must be responsible for that evil either directly or—as theologians have phrased it—permissively. Then there arises the problem known as theodicy, the question of how to justify the goodness of God when God either directly brings about evil or at least appears to permit evil to exist.

This traditional Western conception of deity—this classical theism—also teaches that God exists *from the divine* and *of the divine;* aseity is taken to be the root attribute of the divine. God is not dependent in any sense upon anything else for divine perfection, and a relationship to anything else is not a necessity of God's nature. So God is both self-existent and self-contained. Whatever relationships exist between God and what God creates are only on the side of the creation and in no fashion integral to God's own divine existence. Thomas Aquinas was one of the architects of the Christian West's conception of deity, and he was prepared to say that God's relation to the world is simply logical: God is the logically necessary ground of, and the logical reason for, all contingency or creaturehood. But Aquinas also said that creation's relationship to God is one of total dependence, that the world would not exist at all if God were not creator or cause.

Moreover, in this Western theistic tradition, or in classical theism, God is said to be perfect in the sense that God is complete in God's own self, subsisting eternally without temporality or time sequence as part of the divine being. God's perfection is seen in the divine changelessness, immutability, impassibility, and eternity. There is no "becoming" in God; God simply is. Nothing changes in God or for God. God is not genuinely affected by what goes on in creation; nothing that happens in the world can influence God one way or another. God is above and beyond suffering, too, since suffering in all its forms is taken to be the mark of imperfection, creatureliness, alteration, or contingency. Thus in the divine essential being, God is absolute. This sort of interpretation of perfection, adopted very early in the development of classical theism, has its origin in the insistence of Greek philosophy that perfection simply *means* changelessness or immutability. Any other notion of perfection was ruled out from the start.

This conception of God is basically Hellenistic in origin, but with it Christian theologians have sought to combine the Jewish emphasis upon God as righteous moral will. That is to say, they wanted to bring the ethical insight of the Jewish tradition, found preeminently in the Hebrew prophets, into the Hellenistic insistence on changelessness, immutability, and impassibility. The marriage was not easy to accomplish, but nonetheless it was finally brought about in such a way that it stood up for a long period, indeed, from about the third century onward to the end of the nineteenth. And God's righteous moral will was interpreted after the Jewish view that God had given commandments, which were to be accepted and obeyed without question. If they were thus obeyed, rewards would be given to the creatures; if they were not obeyed, punishment would be meted out. But in all cases, God was not affected by what went on in the world.

Again, we may notice that the model used to picture God in much popular religious talk, and in some theological talk too, was borrowed, as Whitehead noted in his *Modes of Thought* (Free Press, 1968, p. 49), from "the characteristics of the touchy, vain, imperious tyrants who ruled the empires of the world." Consequently, the notion of God is as of a dictator; and "our modern rituals," as Whitehead goes on to say in the same passage, "still retain this taint." Yet, as we shall see below, the four Gospels (along with some Buddhist teaching) contain what the same writer rightly styled "the most emphatic repudiations of this archaic notion."

Thus the traditional conception of deity, which we have

received from our past, puts its main stress on divine absoluteness or aseity; on divine causative agency as the explanation of everything that occurs whether by direct divine willing or by indirect divine permission with respect to evil
done in the world; on divine self-containedness and hence
lack of necessary relationship with anything else; on divine
impassibility, which makes any suffering impossible for
God; and on divine moral perfection, with the giving of
laws in accordance with which everything should be ordered.   Even up to this point, it is not entirely consistent.
But the theologians who worked out this conception were
also devoted Christians who centered their own religious
faith upon Jesus of Nazareth, for them the very incarnation
of God in human existence.   They believed that Jesus had
come as God in human form and that by his coming, and
above all by his suffering, death, and resurrection, he had
saved God's children from their unfortunate condition of sin
and their resultant alienation from God.   In so doing they
were convinced that God had disclosed or manifested the in-
nermost divine character, nature, and purpose.

That introduced still another contradictory factor.   For the
insight of Christian faith, centered in Jesus, is that because
in this man God was active for human redemption, God was
revealed for what God is.   As 1 John puts it, "God is love."
Therefore, in some fashion love must also be an element in
the divine reality; indeed, it must be the *central* element, or
else the significance of the life of Jesus, his death, and his renewed life in resurrection would be denied.   Right here,
then, we come to the further and very strange contradiction
that runs through traditional Christian versions of classical
theism.   On the one hand, we have a conception of deity as
absolute, immutable, impassible, without essential relationships, self-existent and self-contained.   On the other hand,
we have a conception of God as both morally righteous and
supremely loving.   It *might* have been possible to affirm
moral righteousness along with Hellenistic absoluteness;
after all, it is not beyond our imagining that a kind of moral
tyranny, with a calculus of rewards and punishments, could

be ascribed to an entirely absolute being. But when it comes to *love*, things are very different. Love is relationship; it knows anguish as well as joy; it enters into and participates in the life of the beloved; it is even, as Whitehead once put it, "a little oblivious as to morals." Certainly it can never be entirely self-contained. Love depends on those whom it loves; it is influenced by them and always affected by them, although if it is true love it never falters in its faithfulness in loving.

We can see in many of the greatest Christian thinkers just this ambiguity or contradiction. In Origen, the Alexandrian theologian of the third century, there is found both Hellenistic or Platonizing thought *and* deep Christian faith in God's love. So also with Augustine, the North African whose writings have been more influential than those of any other ancient writer in subsequent Western theology. Thomas Aquinas tried to combine an acceptance of Aristotelian concepts with equally profound Christian conviction. In Luther, the philosophical aspect is in principle rejected, or at least deposed from its central place; but it remains implicit in his double stress on the mysterious will of the "terrible" God (God's *opus alienum*, "strange work," in a world of evil and sin) *and* God's "gracious" will (God's *opus proprium*, personal action in love). In Calvin, voluntarism gets the upper hand; God is conceived as absolute will, and yet God is also said to love and care for humankind.

This long discussion of so-called classical theism in its Christian version will have served its purpose if it helps us to understand the reason for the violent antitheistic movements of recent times and to see why some serious thinkers have even said that God is dead. The antitheistic movement is directed against the conception of God that may be styled roughly as metaphysical absolutism. The death-of-God school tells us that the picture of God we have just outlined, save for its inclusion of love and moral justice when modified by love, has died on those who have discovered the reality of human freedom, the human capacity to act significantly, and the responsibility we have for acting in freedom.

The process thinkers of our time who have turned their attention to the religious question—the process theologians, as they are usually called—are sure, however, that there is another and sounder conception of God, one which makes love the clue to the divine nature and manner of working in the world and one which is also in accordance with what we know to be going on in that world.

Thus, instead of emphasizing aseity, or self-containedness as well as sheer self-existence, as God's essential nature, such theologians give the central place to love-in-action, which presupposes and entails relationships. Instead of perfection as unchangeableness or immutability, they speak of perfection as love in its highest and fullest degree, adapting itself unceasingly to concrete situations. Instead of impassibility or absence of suffering, they point to Calvary as a disclosure of God as "suffering love." Instead of an absolute being uninfluenced by anything else, they stress God's relationship with the world. Instead of making "being itself" their final description of God, they recognize a dynamic "becoming" as integral to the divine nature. They do not interpret the divine righteousness in starkly moralistic terms; rather, they see that righteousness is also a mode of God's love, a love whose faithfulness and persistence are shown in the adamant way in which the lover wants the very best, and only that, from those who are loved.

It ought to be apparent that in most respects this conception of God, which Charles Hartshorne has called "neoclassical theism" or "the di-polar conception of God," is a natural consequence of the more general process way of seeing things or looking at the world. In Whitehead's words, God is taken to be not "the great exception" to everything else but the "chief exemplification" of whatever the necessary interpretative principles for everything are. Dynamism, interrelationship, "energetic activity" and "emotional intensity," a working toward the actualizing of aims or goals, and a striving to use what the past offers in order to achieve fulfillment, which includes overcoming twistings, backwaters, lags, and selfishly made decisions in the creation we know—this is how the world goes. And this provides a context for a conception of God in which God is seen as supreme persuasion working for "victory over force," as love in its self-giving, its self-identifying, and its receptivity. The freedom for decision in the creation makes those who are created causative agents also, so that God is the *chief* causative agency not the *only* one, whose action makes possible, and also is affected by, the creaturely decisions that (in Whitehead's phrase) "matter and have consequences."

This conception of God can readily find a place for the disclosure of God in the event of Christ. In a way, as Professor A.H. Johnson has suggested, it is nothing other than a generalization from that event, a generalization applied to the rest of experience and to the world where we live. "Supernaturalism," in the sense of God's making known the divine only by divine intrusions from outside in occasional miraculous acts, is rejected; a picture of deity as remote and inaccessible is refuted; and the condemnation of secular activities as a blasphemous denial of the divine prerogative is entirely ruled out. So also is worship or prayer when these are regarded as a "pestering of the deity," in Dean Inge's biting words, or as primarily a cringing submission to an absolute will. Nor is moral behavior seen as simple conformity to external rules imposed from above without regard for those upon whom they are imposed. Instead of all these, we have a portrayal of deity as organically related to the world, indeed, supremely related, because God is supremely the cosmic Lover. And we have an interpretation of human existence as a movement toward love, accepted willingly or rejected selfishly with the inevitable consequences of human fulfillment or nonfulfillment. We have a moral vision in which humankind is called to respond to the lure of the divine love under human conditions, a vision about which we have had much to say earlier.

For this new theism, the significance of Jesus is found first in his providing the classical instance of what is always and everywhere operative, although it is working against serious obstacles that yet cannot defeat the cosmic thrust toward loving and sharing. Second, in Jesus there is also the special focusing of the persuasive activity of cosmic Love to work in the world to redeem it, or bring it to its intended fulfillment. And that world can now be understood as the field for Love's action. Thus, the process theologian can agree with W.H. Auden that space is the "where" and time the "when" in which we can learn to love. If this conception of deity is accepted, then a radical reconception of many aspects of the inherited Christian theological scheme is demanded. Contemporary process theologians are now concerning themselves with this task.

To a large degree, these theologians have followed Whitehead's thought, but they have also used the thought of Charles Hartshorne, the contemporary American philosopher whom I have quoted earlier and who has developed Whiteheadian themes and added some of his own. With a dozen books to his credit, Hartshorne has devoted most of his attention to the exposition of what he calls a "di-polar" view of deity. In one sense, he says, God is absolute and perfect, since God is *always* loving, *always* faithful, *always* Love; but in another sense, God is relative, since the divine absolute perfection consists precisely in God's never-failing adaptation of self-giving to and self-identifying with the world and in God's ceaseless receptivity from that world. This entails a complete reinterpretation of the meaning of absoluteness and perfection, to be sure, but certainly we need not suppose that the Hellenistic identification of these with immutability and impassibility is a final definition.

In such books as *Beyond Humanism, Man's Vision of God, A Natural Theology for Our Time, Creative Synthesis and Philosophic Method*, and *The Logic of Perfection*, Hartshorne has been indefatigable in the presentation of this "di-polar" position. He has given process theologians a body of work that along with Whitehead's writings provides them with a clearly argued and lucidly stated philosophical basis for theological reconstruction.

This is not the place to list fully the many books that have been written by process theologians, most of them in North America but some in Britain, the continent of Europe, and Australia. Many are listed in the bibliography appended to my *Process Thought and Christian Faith* (Nisbet, 1968), and an almost complete list is given in *Process Philosophy and Christian Thought* (Bobbs-Merrill, 1971). But I must mention especially a work by the late Daniel Day Williams called *The Spirit and the Forms of Love* (Nisbet, 1968); this is a full-length presentation of a process-theology systematic, soundly argued, eminently readable, and deeply Christian in tone.

It has sometimes been said that process theology is only a passing fad which will make no lasting contribution to the Christian world. But the mere fact that so many thinkers have written so many books on the subject shows that this criticism is invalid. What is more, for well over thirty years process theology has been a vigorous Christian movement. First in the United States, then in France, Italy, Spain, and Latin America, more recently in Holland, Belgium, and Germany, and now at last in Great Britain, serious attention is being paid to its work, not least among Roman Catholics who are impatient with the older Thomism, which for so long has been quasi-official in that communion, and who are looking for a conceptuality which will be comprehensive in its sweep, open to newer knowledge and science, and available for Christian use. This they believe they have found in the writings of Whitehead and to a lesser degree in those of Hartshorne.

If it be true, as John A.T. Robinson urged a decade ago in *Honest to God*, that we must have a new image of God, then it may well be that process thinking will give us what we need. Robinson himself has found this to be the case, as his more recent books *Exploration into God* and *The Human Face of God* demonstrate. A conception of God as "in the world, or nowhere, creating continually in and around us," as Whitehead put it toward the end of his life, is the starting place for any viable revision of the divine image. Scientific understanding, humane appreciation, existentialist self-awareness, history as cumulative experience, psychological insight, and respectful regard for what religious people have to tell us about their experience—all are needed for and capable of inclusion in this new perspective.

Mother Julian of Norwich, that remarkable English mystic of the Middle Ages, tells us she heard God saying these words to her, and they sum up much of what in less beautiful idiom we have just been urging:

> See! I am God. See! I am in all thing. See! I do all thing. See! I never lift my hands off my works, nor ever shall, without end. See! I lead all thing to the end I ordained it from without beginning, by the same might, wisdom, and love whereby I made it.

This would seem a remarkable anticipation of process theology's vision of God, which will be presented in detail in Part Two.

PART TWO

God in Process: Christian Faith and Process Thought

8

Christian Faith in God

Many definitions of Christianity have been proposed, both in scholarly theological volumes and in books of more popular appeal. Christianity has been described as a set of beliefs about God and humankind and as a way of life; or attention has been centered on the worship of God through Christ. For our purposes, the most satisfactory definition would be: Christianity is the total life of the community of men and women who respond to what they know about God —along with their neighbors, who are caught up into the social movement or process we call "the church" (however this may be understood)—in terms of the socially remembered event of Jesus Christ. Each person who wishes to be called Christian has a share in this community. Christianity is thus a great movement in history, from the first preaching of Jesus as Lord continuing on through the ages, enriched by the insight and experience of countless people who have taken part in the process. It is a dynamic and living community, whose members are united in a common allegiance and common response to Jesus as the community both remembers him and proclaims his significance.

That dynamic and living fellowship has always been marked by certain distinctive characteristics. It has explained its allegiance and response to Jesus as Lord by talking about his significance in relation to the supreme reality we call God and to the humanity that Jesus shared with us. It has found its central expressive action in a specific kind of worship—the eucharistic remembrance of Jesus' life and death and continuing activity in the world. It has made possible for the members of the fellowship a "life in Christ," as the New Testament calls it, in which the presence and work of that Lord are still felt to be active in the world. Basically, Christianity is a social movement that follows from a relationship to the divine reality, mediated by and made available through Jesus Christ as in some vitalizing fashion he is experienced and served in the society that bears his name.

Thus Christianity is a *faith*. It is not essentially a philosophy or an ordered system of ideas; neither is it merely a kind of behavior that imitates the earthly life and teaching of a historical figure. It is a commitment of men and women to the supremely worshipful reality called God, as this reality is believed to disclose itself to us, but it is not an individualistic commitment, since it demands full participation, to a greater or lesser degree, in a corporate experience conveyed through the ages by a community of men and women drawn from the most varied backgrounds and races, classes, nations, and cultures. In a sense one might say that the corporate faith of the fellowship is more important than that of any individual in it, yet that is not quite true, for each of those individuals—or, better, *persons*—makes his or her own contribution to the total community of faith, while the community's faith deepens, enriches, develops, and corrects the faith of the believer. That is why we rightly say "*We* believe," rather than rest content with "I believe." *I* do indeed believe, but I believe as one of a great company of men and women, from many ages, of all races and classes, rich and poor, simple and learned, who in one way or another have been drawn to find the truest key to the meaning and purpose of human existence given focal expression in Jesus Christ.

This also is the reason that every Christian must of necessity be "high church," not in any denominational sense, not with any ecclesiastical overtones, but simply because to be a Christian at all—as we have defined it—means to be a member of that great community of Christian life and worship and faith which has come to be known as "the church." The fellowship, properly understood, is part of the total Christian "thing" because it is the essential carrier of the Christian way; nobody can be a Christian entirely on his or her own, although every Christian who is at all serious about the profession of the name of Christ must exert every effort to be a loyal disciple and a faithful member of the fellowship.

The faith of a Christian is essentially faith in Jesus Christ—a commitment to him and a trust in him. But as we have just seen, a Christian's faith is also the faith of the Christian community. It would be better to say that the basic faith of a Christian is faith *in God apprehended and available in Jesus Christ,* for it is God, the divine reality we shall speak about in this chapter, who is at the center. Yet it is also true that Christianity is unique in its conviction that God and Jesus are inextricably linked together: God in Christ, Christ manifesting God, God made real to us in the man Jesus. Here are the enduring affirmations of the specifically Christian way of faith.

Faith means commitment to God. To say "we believe" is to say that for all eternity we put our whole trust, our complete confidence, our final reliance, in the divine reality made available to us in Jesus Christ. Such faith is "the master light of all our seeing," the sheet anchor of our lives, the dominant element in the whole existence of the Christian person. But it is not contrary to our knowledge, it is not believing what is not so. There is nothing irrational about being a Christian and placing one's trust in God manifested in Christ. Of course, the Christian's faith goes beyond the *merely* rational; there is a "leap," to use Kierkegaard's word, but it is not a blind leap. Someone has defined faith as "reason grown courageous," and this apt phrase gives us the clue to the relationship between human rational powers and the act of belief.

There is, in fact, plenty of evidence that points toward the reality of God and that makes reasonable the Christian claim about Jesus Christ. The universe would make no sense if there were not some chief causative agency, some source of novelty, some final destiny, some creative and energizing activity striving for the accomplishment of great ends. And the impact of Jesus Christ upon history, his continuing influence and power in the world, the very wonder of his person itself that we read about in the New Testament—all point to his being more than the best of men, making credible the conviction stated in a hymn, that in Jesus we have "God in man made manifest." But we can no more say that this is the case than we can say that God is active and living Love, without going beyond what "reason alone" (to use Kant's phrase) can tell us.

Yet once the venture of faith has been made, in company with the great band of men and women who have held that faith, we can find that the venture is confirmed in experience. Stability, purpose, empowering of life, a sense of release and acceptance—all follow upon the venture. As the old Latin saying has it, *solvitur ambulando:* it is proved to us and for us in the very act of accepting it and living by it. So much of pragmatism is inevitable and essential. "You will know them by their fruits," said Jesus, and the fruits of continuing acts of self-commitment are plain in lives made whole and right, given purpose and meaning.

One of the tragedies of Christian history has been the way in which some in positions of leadership have sought to turn the great dynamic movement of Christian faith and living into an ignorant obscurantism. They have fought advances of thought, they have tried to defeat the efforts of men and women to know more about the world, they have denied the validity of scientific truth, they have called into question the freedom and responsibility, as well as the dignity, of human life. But despite their unhappy efforts, the Christian fellowship has never finally been willing to remain in some outworn position or rest content in some backwater, for there have always been those who pushed forward in the certain confidence that God is the God of truth and that nothing that is true can deny the disclosure of the divine self given in Jesus Christ. It is and always has been possible to be a modern person, living the life of one's own time, and also a convinced Christian. This reverent modernism is the only true orthodoxy; the other variety of orthodoxy is a dead and ineffective traditionalism, in the worst sense of that much-abused and yet invaluable word.

None of us knows the whole truth; we humans will never know it, short of seeing God, who *is* Truth. We know in part, yet that which we know, as honest and reverent Christian believers, is right and sound. It needs, however, constantly to be related to the rest of our knowledge, in the many human fields of research, study, and experience. The task of the thoughtful Christian is found precisely at this point. That Christian must see all life in light of this central vision and, conversely, must see this central vision in the light of all the rest that is known and seen. Constant rethinking, constant reinterpretation, and never-ending restatement are involved in this task. Yet the basic certainties stand sure; they concern the dynamic reality who is God, God's pervasive action in the world, God's self-manifestation through the whole range of creation, God's focal self-expression in Jesus Christ, the effecting of God's purpose through loving activity in the world and in human existence, and the assurance that our human life is not an end in itself but finds its fulfillment through reception into the divine life.

When one thinks of the great Christian community, in its long history and its wide reach, in all its variety and inclusiveness, one is filled with reverence and a sense of the mystery of corporate faith, worship, and life. Every parish and every mission, no matter how small and insignificant it may seem, no matter how picayune and narrow its concerns may appear, has its part in this historical movement. And when one is despondent about one's own St. John's-by-the-Sea, one can turn again and again from that congregation and its apparent failure to the great fellowship through the ages and find in the thought of that fellowship a cordial for drooping spirits. There is more here than meets the eye, and one's local congregation is a participant in that family of faith which endures through the centuries as what Paul called the Body of Christ.

But the only way in which one can be a participant in that great tradition is through a willing sharing in the small cell of the Body in the place where one happens to live—and such willing sharing will have the double effect of strengthening both one's own faith and the community of faith. It will make more effectual the witness of the apparently insignificant and ineffective local congregation, at which it is easy enough to sneer if one is so inclined. However, if we are humbly though critically ready to put up with the fellowship in its particular local manifestation, where and as we find it, we shall help to renew and strengthen it, at the same time discovering for ourselves the deepening of Christian discipleship and finding that we are enriched by other men and women who, like ourselves, are seeking to live in the Christian way, informed by the Christian faith, and supported by Christian worship.

We have said that the faith of a Christian is a shared self-commitment to God in utter trust and confidence. And we have noted that such a definition must at once be qualified by the addition of the phrase "revealed in Jesus Christ" after the word God. For Christianity is no bare theism. Even the modern Unitarian, insofar as he or she would make claim to the Christian name whatever may be thought about theological definitions of Jesus Christ's significance, will say that his or her religion is toward God as God is defined by Jesus Christ—which is to say that the specifically Christian understanding of God must be in terms of what Whitehead styled "the Galilean vision."

In much conventional Christian thinking, preaching, and teaching, God has been presented in ways that are far different from "the God and Father of our Lord Jesus Christ." There has been a presentation of God as the Absolute in a sense that God becomes an almost static being. There has been teaching about God which so emphasizes omnipotence that God seems above good and evil and in any event simply pushes things and people around in an entirely arbitrary manner. There has been talk of God as a moral tyrant, ready to descend with punishment upon those who violate what is supposed to be divine law. There has been a presentation in which a biblical symbol has been pushed to the exclusion of the rest, so that the resultant picture is not adequate to the richness of the biblical witness as it has been developed and modified through centuries of Jewish history. The models used to point to God have often been in horrible apostasy from the vision of pure unbounded love given in the event of Jesus Christ as it has been received and found significant.

What model, then, is the right one? That there must be *some* model is plain enough, since for us humans it is inevitable that we grasp the invisible, supreme, worshipful, divine reality in terms drawn from our own experience *as* humans. The distinctively Christian model—although anticipations of it, intimations and hints, and sometimes fairly vivid representations are found elsewhere—can be stated very simply: God is the cosmic Lover. So the basic Christian affirmation is that God is both the creative energy in all things, whose sovereign rule includes the whole world in its sweep, and also the living God who can and does enter into relationship with creation. But above all God is Love, Love-in-act, loving Action. God is the divine reality without whom there would be no world such as we know. God is also the one who communicates in love something of the divine self to that world, identifying with it, disclosing the divine self in many ways to men and women, working to bring them to the knowledge and love of God that is their own wholeness and their true life.

This picture of God is central to the scriptural picture, as Old Testament understanding comes to fulfillment in New Testament discernment. And as we have seen in Part One, the modern conceptuality known as process thought adds rational confirmation to just that picture. But if such be the case, this means that the conventional list of divine attributes is in need of thorough revision, or at the least careful reinterpretation.

Take as an example the word omnipotence. It is not in itself descriptive of God as God is portrayed in the Bible. Years ago, a friend of mine ventured to write an illuminating essay in which he urged—and I believe with complete success—that the power of God, as it is envisaged in Scripture, is properly defined as "ability to accomplish that which God purposes" and not as "ability to do anything whatsoever." Hence we shall do well to think of the divine omnipotence as meaning cosmic Love's supreme capacity to work in and through, as well as with, the world, indefatigably and indefeasibly. In other words, God as Love is the only *genuinely* strong reality. God is *pantocrator*, as the Greek has it, "all-ruler"—and "all-ruler" in divine sovereign love. The divine omnipresence means the divine Love's universal action; the divine omniscience means the divine Love's awareness of the depths and heights of possibility; the divine transcendence means the divine Love's utter inexhaustibility; the divine immanence means the divine Love's unfailing presence. And to call God infinite is not to say that God is absolutely unlimited or to think of God as entirely beyond our knowing. Rather, it is to say that God's *Love* knows no limit and that God reveals the divine self to creation as precisely Love, but does this out of that limitless Love which is the divine self.

By saying "God," religion intends to point toward the divine reality, the chief causative agency in the world, the supreme responsive agency to the world's ongoing process, the ultimate recipient of what is accomplished in the world. As supreme, and as supremely Love, God is altogether worshipful and adorable. But the adjectives that must be used to describe this divine reality are "living," "responsive," "communicative," "related," and (as I have urged) above all "loving." God is alive with a fullness of life and vibrancy of selfhood that far exceed anything we know in our own experience. God is the Life which moves through all that is not the divine self. God is a rich unity capable of getting in touch with what is not the divine self while possessing the freedom to be the divine self. Our own meager understanding of personality is not adequate to describe this truth about God. We could, and perhaps we should, speak of God as "super-personal," were it not that such a term might suggest that God is impersonal rather than more-than-personal-as-we-know-it.

To speak about God is to speak of the eternal Goodness, in the phrase from the *Theologica Germanica*, which Luther loved so much. God is not neutral about the issues of life. The divine righteousness is the capacity, the power, and the will to set right what is wrong; to bring good out of evil, right out of wrong; to establish the right conditions in the world and thus to accomplish God's loving intention. God's sovereign rule over creation is such that this intention cannot in the long run suffer defeat, however much evil, wrong, and sin there may be in the world as we now see and experience it.

But God is not responsible for that evil, wrong, and sin. God neither directly wills it nor permissively allows it. To talk in that fashion, as have many theologians over the centuries, is to misunderstand two things. First, it is to fail to see that the creatures, including you and me and whatever else is not God, have their own degree of freedom and their own capacity for choices that may be good or bad, upbuilding or destructive. God is *chief* cause, to be sure, but God is not the only cause. And created causes are genuine causes, not imitation ones; as such, they have consequences. Second, God deals with the evil, wrong, and sin by the suffering love that can mysteriously transmute it into good. Of this the cross of Jesus Christ is the sign and symbol. What is more, God calls humanity to be co-workers with God in overcoming evil, wrong, and sin by our devotion, vigorous effort, and willing response to what we know of God's love and God's purpose for us.

God is no remote deity. As living and personal, God is *in* the world. We might even also say that the world is in God. This position is to be distinguished from pantheism, in which God and the world are practically identical. Professor Charles Hartshorne has suggested that the right word for God's relation to the creation is "panentheism," a term first used in the mid-nineteenth century and taken up by Baron Friedrich von Hügel fifty years ago. "Everything-in-God" tells us that God is not so exalted that he becomes meaningless to human life, but rather is operative in the whole creation at every level, moving through it, working upon it, accomplishing the divine goodwill in it. God is "closer to us than breathing, nearer than hands or feet."

At the same time, God is not exhausted or used up by self-identification with the world. We can draw an analogy from our own experience and see that as we are *in* our activity but are yet *more than* any particular action, with reserves of energy upon which we may draw, so God is *in* the divine operation in creation—indeed that operation is itself divine—but God is not *lost* in it. When we say that God is transcendent, we are affirming just this. If we get away from silly notions of a spatial transcendence, in which God is (so to speak) "out there" and which is in effect the God of eighteenth-century Deism, we shall be able to maintain with the Old Testament that God is "the high and lofty One who inhabits eternity," yet is also near to us, with us, in us, and for us. To put it simply, God is the unexhausted and inexhaustible divine reality who works through all things yet ever remains God.

In the historic passage, as well as in human experience, God is active. In the strange and bewildering complex of human willing and action, God moves through lure and attraction to bring the greatest good out of the confusion of human events. God is accomplishing a purpose there, although there is no reason to assume that there is an inevitable, almost automatic, progress going on. Often, even in the long run, we do not see God's purpose being fulfilled. But it is precisely faith in God that leads us to believe that God's ends will be achieved and that God calls humanity to be divine co-workers, to be God's personal instruments or agents who, in our freedom and with our human dignity, can play a part in the divine sovereign rule. What we do *counts,* not only for us and for the human future but also for and to God's self.

Finally, God is self-consistent. God adapts to what goes

on in the world through creaturely decision—the Bible portrays this in pictorial fashion, time and again—and values those decisions and can use them. But God is faithful. God does not contradict the divine self, is true to the divine intention, loyal to the divine character, acting always in ways that are congruous with the divine final goal of the rule of love.

This is why the popular conception of the miraculous, as divine intrusion into and manipulation of the world, is contrary not only to our modern understanding of how things in fact go there but also to the deepest meaning of the scriptural witness. Doubtless the Bible tells of many miracles, but the basic point of each story is that God is the living God who works to accomplish the divine purposes. The unnatural side of the miracle stories is a reflection not of the basic scriptural witness to God but of the unscientific notions of the several writers. In any event, the biblical words that are translated "miracle" in most of our English versions mean "sign" (*semeion*), manifestation of divine energy (*dunamis*), and that which surprises us and makes us wonder (*terrha*). These are the New Testament Greek words; the Old Testament Hebrew terms are similar in meaning. Everything in the Jewish and Christian understanding of God would be lost if God were thought to be a static and inert being rather than the living deity who acts in nature, history, and human experience. But nothing is lost and much is gained when our grasp of the truth about God's living action in these areas precludes the thought that God intervenes to violate the internal congruity and consistency of the divine creation with its never-absent divine energizing in and through created entities, events, and happenings. As far as we can see from our own experience and observation, and by analogy in the ongoing of nature, God does not break into and act contrary to the creation's continuity, although God does lure that creation to produce genuine novelty.

Professor A.E. Taylor wrote many years ago that no living religion could do without the idea of the supernatural, by which he meant God as more than human or created, but that it did not require the idea of the miraculous. Supernatural may not have been a happy word; I think that it was not. But Taylor was correct in rejecting miracle as a necessity in religious thinking. When we have become intellectually mature enough to give up childish notions of divine intrusions and rescue expeditions, even with respect to Jesus himself (about whom we speak in the next chapter), and to trust in God who is revealing the divine self as actively energizing within the world, we shall be able to have a more soundly based and more credible view of the divine reality.

This view of God and God's ways in the world does not make prayer impossible, as some have said. There is a sub-Christian idea of prayer that thinks we can twist God's will to our own ends. But prayer is basically the surrender and exposure of ourselves to God, so that God may work the divine way with us and in us: "Not as I will, but as thou wilt." Prayer is the lifting of ourselves to God, so that God may fill us with and use us for the divine self—and for our own great good. In that experience we are cleansed of distortions in our willing and desiring, and we are made to be the true men and women we are intended to be. Through our surrender to God, God is able to do great things. There is no limit to what our prayer can accomplish, as Dr. W.P. DuBose, the American theologian of the early years of this century, once said; but (he went on to say) it is always in us and through us, not entirely in spite of us or by means that are contrary to the consistency of the divine operation itself.

What has been said in this chapter represents, however briefly and inadequately, what the deepest Christian faith in God is concerned to affirm. It is appropriate that we close the chapter by preparing for what shall be said in the next about him who is taken in that faith to be our clue to the nature of the divine reality as well as the clue to the humanity he shared with us.

From what has been urged above we see that God's activity in the world is not confined to the historical person of Jesus Christ; incarnation is "the manner and the mode," in Cardinal Bérulle's words, of all God's working in the world, which we find vividly disclosed in "the Galilean vision."

God is ever incarnating the divine self in creation, ever entering into it. It is not as if God were absent from it and then intervened in it now and again; in the more profound sense, the unexhausted divine self ever energizes in nature and history, and above all in the lives of men and women, expressing that self in such a fashion that the whole created order is in one sense God's body. It is a matter of the divine reality working in and with created reality. In differing ways, with varying degrees of intensity, God expresses the divine self by activity, which, as we shall see in the next chapter, is nothing other than God in the worldward relationship. Something of God is shown in the natural order, more in living matter, and still more in the movement in history toward righteousness, justice, beauty, and goodness. Above all, in the personalities of men and women and in their concrete historical circumstances, God is at work. God is disclosed as the ground of being, the creative energy that maintains order and provides novelty, the lure toward realizing possibilities. God's activity in the world is the light that lightens every person. It is *all* incarnation, but it is not on a uniformitarian level since there are heights and depths, a more or a less, a here and a there, in the ongoing creative process.

In such a context, against such a background, Christian faith sees in Jesus Christ the appearance of a focus, a specific point, a decisive event. In him the entire movement is crowned, so far as humankind is concerned, with an action that shows the meaning of it all as we humans can grasp it and respond to it. In him we see what God is up to in the world. Through that focusing in one of our own kind, we are given the truth about life, the way to live it, and the kind of living which is humanly worthy and divinely desired. This insight of Christian faith has been expressed in the phrase "the Word became flesh and dwelt among us." Here in Christ is a focal manifestation in human life of God the creative reality, a manifestation in terms of action—and that action is on our human plane and in our human situation, speaking to our human condition.

9

The Self-Expressive
Activity of God and the
Meaning of Jesus Christ

At the heart of Christian faith, Christian worship, and Christian life is the figure of Jesus Christ. He is the Lord whom Christians adore and serve. His person and his teaching provide in some manner the standard for Christian behavior. His Spirit, entering into the lives of those who respond to him, is for the Christian "the power of God for salvation." His is "the name which is above every name." How then are we to interpret him and his significance?

Alfred North Whitehead had some important things to say on this subject. In *Adventures of Ideas* (Cambridge University Press, 1933, p. 170) he said that "the essence of Christianity is the appeal to the life of Christ as a revelation of the nature of God and of God's agency in the world." He went on to say:

The record is fragmentary, inconsistent, and uncertain . . . but there can be no doubt as to what elements in the record have evoked a response from all that is best in human nature. The Mother, the Child, and the bare manger: the lowly man, homeless and self-forgetful, with his message of peace, love, and sympathy: the suffering, the agony, the tender words as life ebbed, the final despair: and the whole with the authority of supreme victory.

As we shall see, it is exactly in this disclosure *in act* (as Whitehead put it in the same passage) of that which others—and for Whitehead chiefly Plato, but we can add many more names—have discerned *in theory*, that the distinctiveness of Christianity lies. The event in history which is indicated when we say "Jesus Christ" has about it an importance that for Christians is supreme and decisive.

Earlier we noted that "importance" has a significant place in process thought. In a universe that is made up not of things but of events or occasions, each of these has integral to it some value in that it is indicative (to greater or less degree) of how things actually go in that world. Every interpretation of the meaning of human experience, every understanding of the world in its totality, must by necessity start from some particular stance—or, better, must find some particular point that is taken to be of special importance among all the events or occasions; it provides a clue to the totality of experience. But it does more: it makes possible new occasions for future creative advance, since it is in terms of that which is taken as important that decision and action in the direction of fulfillment of aim, or realization of possibility, will occur. This is generally true. Our own experience demonstrates that some moment, a particular occurrence (falling in love, getting one's first job, choosing one's vocation, in social matters a special incident in, say, national history like the granting of the Magna Charta in England or the American Revolution for the United States) assumes a decisive role in subsequent events. This point *matters*; in itself it makes an enormous impact on those affected by it. It *has results*; because of it, things happen which otherwise would not have happened.

Now it is the declaration of Christian faith that *the* important event in history, so far as men and women are concerned, is the appearance in the world of Jesus of Nazareth. He is not the *only* important fact, to be sure, for other facts have had their significance for those in differing cultures and with different cultural backgrounds. But for millions Jesus has been, and increasingly becomes for other millions, just that important event, even if they are not in any sense avowed Christians. The fact of Jesus Christ is a fact that is central to the interpretation of the human, and hence also of the cosmic, enterprise, for all occurrences in the human realm have their significance for the wider cosmic setting in which they take place, for good or for ill.

Whitehead said that Jesus is the "revelation in act" of that which Plato and others as well have "discerned" or "divined in theory." What is there revealed is that persuasion not compulsion, love not force, is at the heart of the creative process of the universe. It is this which gives Jesus his central place and role, and it is from this centrality, or particular "importance," in our understanding and in our living, that the evaluation of Jesus himself, his significance in the total scheme of things, his continuing impact on successive generations of men and women, takes its rise.

But in the first instance the evaluation of Jesus was made by his companions and friends. He was taken by them to be a great teacher, the last of the prophets, perhaps even the fulfillment of Israel's hope that God would send a final word to humanity in one known as the Messiah. As Whitehead put it, Christ gave his life; it has been for Christians, first in those earliest days and then in the years following his presence among humankind, to "discern the doctrine"—to discover his significance and to relate him, so far as can be done, to the totality of human experience and to the world in which that experience is had. This is not the place to attempt a full historical sketch of the development of that doctrine. Suffice it to say that it reached its culmination, so far as scriptural witness is concerned, in the affirmation that in Christ the Word (the self-expressive creative Activity which is divine in nature) "became flesh and dwelt among us," while in formal theological statement the climax was the declaration that in him there is a genuine union of divine Activity ("true God") and human activity like our own ("true human being").

Here we have two stories about Jesus made into a unity by the act of Christian faith. As is the case throughout our experience, there is a human story, a naturalistic story if you will. There is a man who was born, lived, taught, suffered, and died. But there is also a divine story, as there can be for every other aspect of human history and human experience. This is the story of what God is up to in that historic, human event. It is an interpretation, certainly, in that it goes beyond the sheer given of the facts as recorded for us in the partial and fragmentary Gospel narratives. But it is an interpretation whose purpose is to make sense of, and give sense to, the facts as they are recorded. It is more, too. It is an interpretation that is intended to make sense of and give sense to the persisting fact that Jesus is not only a figure of the past but in some profoundly real way a present factor in the experience of the human race. Whatever may have been the actual course of events, historically speaking, which the New Testament means to signify when it speaks of the resurrection of Jesus Christ, it is at least clear that it was the conviction of the New Testament writers, building on the testimony of the disciples after the crucifixion of Jesus—as it has been the continuing conviction of millions of Christian people since that time—that far from Jesus' being "put out of the way" by his death at the hands of the Roman authorities in Palestine, he was "let loose into the world." Those phrases are taken from John Masefield's play *The Trial of Jesus*, and they are by no means accidental phrases. In other words, consideration of the significance of Jesus must include reference to what was intended by the narratives, and behind them by the experience, of what is there styled "the resurrection."

Any evaluation of the significance of Jesus must be given in terms appropriate to the general world view of those who seek to make it. The truth that the evaluation contains may indeed be constant, but the ways in which it is to be understood must vary from age to age. And when we have such an overturning of world view as has taken place in the past several hundred years, older formulations will no longer serve the purpose they once did. For example, talk of coming down from heaven may have been appropriate in a world that conceived the divine habitations as almost literally "above"; it will also be appropriate as a useful metaphorical way of describing the presence among us of that which (again in a symbolic sense) is higher than human experience as such. But we need other and more contemporary ways of stating the truth if the abiding meaning is to be brought home to thoughtful persons of our own time. The language of religion is always highly metaphorical—we might also say mythological, imaginative, poetical—and it cannot be taken as if it were a literal story or something similar to straightforward human discourse. Thus, to insist on the uniqueness or speciality of Jesus is one thing, and basic to Christian faith, but to present the meaning of such speciality in our own age requires an idiom different from that which was useful for another age.

It is with such problems that we concern ourselves in this chapter. And it is to such problems that we must necessarily address ourselves when we seek a new conception of the doctrine of Christ today. The following pages represent one attempt to do this, and, as indicated earlier, they are written from the point of view of a supporter of process thought as the most adequate conceptuality available for us today.

There are four affirmations about Jesus Christ that historically have been stressed in Christian faith: (1) Jesus is truly human, bone of our bone and flesh of our flesh, living a human life under the same human conditions any one of us faces—thus Christology, statement of the significance of Jesus, must start "from below," as many contemporary theologians are insisting; (2) Jesus is that one in whom God energizes in a supreme degree, with a decisive intensity; in traditional language he has been styled "the Incarnate Word of God"; (3) for our sake, to secure human wholeness of life as it moves onward toward fulfillment, Jesus not only lived among us but also was crucified for us—this is the point of talk about atonement wrought in and by him; (4) death was not the end for him, so it is not as if he never existed at all; in some way he triumphed over death, or was given victory over it, so that now and forever he is a reality in the life of God and effective among humankind. In what follows I shall speak of each of these affirmations and their meaning for Christians today, putting them in the setting provided by the process conception of the divine Activity in the world.

1. *Jesus lived among us as a true human being.* Integral to the Christian understanding of Jesus is that he was genuinely human, living among us as one of us. As it was for the first disciples, so it must be for us; we start with what we can know about Jesus in the reality of his humanity, although we cannot stop there if we allow ourselves to be grasped by the energizing of God that took place in him.

It was perhaps inevitable that the overwhelming experience of God's working made available to men and women in the event of Jesus Christ would lead to a less vigorous insistence on his human personhood. Just such a failure has marked a good deal of Christian history and theology. Yet this failure to stress to the full the reality of that humanity, in all its royal splendor and with all its necessary limitations, has led to an impoverishment of Christianity in age after age. It is indeed only within the last hundred years or so that the thinking of Christians has been able to give full value to that humanity, although the church officially has always resisted theologians who have denied it. We might even say that the Spirit who in mysterious ways seems to guide the Christian fellowship has in our own time (and in the few decades before that time) led us into a fuller apprehension of this truth, as it has "taken of the things of Christ and declared them unto us."

Yet we face a problem here. The Gospels are not biographies, such as we possess for many other historical personages; neither do they give us a consistent and completely accurate record of what occurred. Whitehead remarked that "the record is fragmentary, inconsistent, and uncertain";

and every contemporary New Testament scholar would agree with this judgment. What we have in *all* the Gospels is a "remembrance" of Jesus; but that remembrance is recounted in terms of what he had already become as Lord for those who told the story. This does not imply that there has been willful fabrication in the record, but it does make it necessary for the reader to allow for the ways in which the felt significance of any series of happenings will inevitably be seen and reported. There was a time when, in the early days of New Testament study, it was assumed that by the use of critical method "the quest for the historical Jesus" would be rewarded by a portrayal of that historical figure exactly as he was. That time is now long past, and even the "new quest," as it is called, makes no such claims—its claims are that there is a continuity between the portrayal of Jesus in the Gospels and the ways in which decision is today and always required of those who recognize his own "decisive" quality, which (they believe) *can* be recovered by us.

With this caveat, and along with it the honest admission that the material in the Gospels is not the kind that permits us (after the fashion of earlier "liberal" Protestantism) to pay Jesus what we might style moral compliments—as if he is indubitably known as in every sense, both in teaching and in behavior, to be ideally perfect—we can go on to consider his humanity, insofar as it can be recovered from the impressions of him found in the New Testament. What matters here is that the total *witness* found in the Gospels, as well as in the epistles of Paul, John, and others, is to an activity of God in human existence and through a human activity, through which "newness of life" has been known; God has been seen as sheer Love-in-action, and human existence has been given meaning and value as a potential agency for divine Love in the world and in human affairs.

Jesus lived as *a* man. He cannot properly be described simply as "Man," as if there were some ideal humanity he shared without sharing also in the personalization of humanity true of each of us. He was *a* human being. He lived at a given place, at a given time; he shared the presuppositions, the knowledge, and the cultural milieu proper to such a person. He was a Jew of the first century of our era.

This means, of course, that he was not omniscient any more than he was omnipresent. His knowledge, proper to someone of his time and place and doubtless with that "plus" which attaches to all genius, was the knowledge of a Jew of his age, as were his ways of thinking and teaching. There was much that he did not know, as he himself is reported to have said. What he *did* know in the realm of human knowledge was after the pattern of his own time and place. If he believed, as it seems he did, in disease as caused by supernatural beings called demons, that does not mean we also must believe this. If he read the signs of the times in the eschatological symbolism of his own day, that does not mean that we must so interpret them. His scientific knowledge was not ours. We need not hesitate to say that in these matters he was mistaken. In his physical condition, of course, he was fully a human being. His body and his mind were human; the church was wise enough to condemn as a heresy the Docetic notion that his body was not really human and the Apollinarian view that his human mind was supplanted by the divine Word. It is in the integrity of a full humanity, and in every range of it, that God's action is to be found—God energizes in this man, in his total and genuine personhood, not in some special part of that personhood or by replacing with deity some particular area of human nature.

What is ultimately significant about Jesus is what God did in him and through him. His human life, as we shall see, was an adequate instrument, thoroughly personalized, for God's eternal Word or Self-Expression. The Gospels give us a picture of one who wore our humanity as a royal garment; they show one who was obedient to what he took to be the will, purpose, or intention of God for him. They portray him as in all things responding to the will of his heavenly parent, his existence filled to the brim—and overflowing—with the positive, creative goodness that is God in action. They speak of him as a human person, as a human being is meant to be; we may put this by saying that in Jesus the image of God is supremely emergent and active in genuine manhood.

We cannot demonstrate from the Gospels that at every point and in every moment there was just this response of Jesus as person to God's activity toward him and in him. Such a statement is part of the interpretation of his human existence. It is a way of understanding *how* there could be in Jesus the union of God's activity and the activity of a human being—in traditional language, how the Incarnation (as the church came to call this union) could take place and how in fact it did take place. But there is nothing in the Gospels to contradict that interpretation, even if it is impossible to make it a matter of clear demonstration.

When approached in this fashion, the stories that the earliest Christians told about Jesus and that were later written down have a much richer meaning than when taken in a literalistic fashion. They are intent on showing that here, in Jesus, the Love which *is* God is decisively at work—healing, helping, strengthening, giving life, and above all bringing into existence a community whose characteristic marks are to be faith, hope, and love. It has been said by Dr. F.C. Burkitt that Jesus was "the true Prometheus who brought the divine fire to men and women." But this was done by God in our own human terms, under our own conditions, and through one of ourselves. Any theology that so widens the gulf between Jesus and other human beings as to suggest that he is an alien intruder into our human situation is to be rejected, not only because it is heretical but more importantly because it makes nonsense of the Gospel record and denies the dignity and reality of that life once lived among us. Yet we can say with the *Theologica Germanica* what a person's right arm is to that person, Jesus was to God, as "the strong Son of God" whom for twenty centuries humankind has declared him to have been.

The extraordinary thing is that while at times we may think that we can sit in judgment upon Jesus, all the while it is really he who judges us. The portrayal of him in the Gospels has made him the world's conscience; as John Stuart

Mill, who was no Christian believer, once dared to say, no better test for human living can be found than so to act that Jesus would approve. In our changing circumstances, we are not called to make a copycat imitation of his life in Palestine; that would be impossible for us. But the Spirit that was in him and worked through him has been released into the world, and that Spirit continues as our inspiration and our judgment. So the historical Jesus becomes the living Christ, but he becomes this without ceasing to be the Man of Nazareth, of whom it was said that his "food" was to do God's will and who was seen, in the fullness of his human life, as the act that showed us God's own picture of what human existence really is and what it is meant to be.

Thus, although divinity is not identical with deity even in Jesus, we may seek God in him, not apart from and in contradiction to his human life but in and under the very conditions of that human life. Or, to put it better, we are to be open to *God's* grasping of us in and through that human life, with that which was accomplished by God in its concreteness. We may prepare for our next section, then, by affirming that, for Christian faith, by the prevenient Action of God a human life was taken and made into the instrument for the gracious divine operation; in more traditional idiom, the eternal Word, Self-Expression of very God, was clothed with a true humanity, crowning the rest of God's work in and for God's human children. This is the true meaning of the oft-stated conviction that Jesus was not only *a* human being, although he most certainly was that, but also *representative* Human Being. The notion of an impersonal personhood, sometimes taught by Anglican divines as a way of putting this truth, is nonsensical and impossible, as well as nonscriptural. But the truth remains that in *this* person, one among his brothers and sisters, we really see *ourselves* as we are being created to become, ourselves as by the empowering influence exerted through Jesus we may indeed come to be.

2. *Incarnate Word of God.* The title of this section is the way the Christian church has traditionally asserted that Jesus is that One in whom God energizes in a supreme degree,

with a decisive intensity, to bring about newness of life for humanity. The Christian fellowship has never been content to speak of Jesus Christ in terms that minimize the reality of God's act in him. In all the theologies of the church, as well as in the experience of Christian people—which is the source of these theologies—Jesus has been seen as in some sense one with the God who is creative power, enduring love, and sovereign ruler. Often the statement has been "Jesus is divine," a phrase that risks confusing Godhead and human personhood, which even in Jesus Christ (as the church has also affirmed) are distinct from each other however intimately united they may be. In our discussion we shall avoid this kind of language.

This conviction that in Jesus there is a decisive action of God in the world has commonly been expressed in Christian history by the term incarnation. At best this is a symbolic way of speaking, and to understand it we must look at the whole God-world relationship. Only in the context of that relationship can we see Jesus as the Lord in whom "very God" does indeed energize in and through "very man." In an earlier chapter this wider relationship was mentioned; here we pursue the matter in more detail.

I have urged that the divine reality we call God is nowhere absent from the creation but works and moves in it all and through it all; it is "informed" by God, without whom it would not be what it is. In this sense God is the ground of all creation. Yet the divine life is not exhausted or used up by this presence and operation in the created order. God is transcendent, perhaps not unlike the way we say that a person transcends and is not exhausted in various actions. To describe this double truth, Christian thinkers, employing terms that have both Jewish and Greek backgrounds, began to speak of the Wisdom and the Word of God "by whom all things were made," which is indeed divine but is not "all" there is of God. Such a conception finds its noblest statement in the first few verses of the Fourth Gospel: "In the beginning was the Word, and the Word was with God, and the Word was God. . . . All things were made through [God], and without [God] was not anything made that was made."

Yet the Fourth Gospel does not stop there. It must go on, because the Christian experience of the fact of Christ, and the fact of the Christian experience of Christ, point to a more profound truth. The knowledge and love of Christ had made it clear to the Christian fellowship that the same Word "by whom all things were made" is also the "light that enlightens" every person in the world and above all is the Word who so energized in and shone through the human life of Jesus their Lord that believers could only speak of him as that One in whom "the Word became flesh and dwelt among us." He was described, then, as the "Incarnate Word of God," "full of grace and truth"—full of divine loving-kindness and power, full of the reality of God.

This was not a deifying of Jesus the Man of Nazareth, like that which took place in pagan cults, in which a hero was exalted more and more to the position of *a* god. On the contrary, it was reached by a continual deepening in the experience of the significance of Jesus' action, in the light of that which he increasingly came to mean to those who committed themselves to him. He was never *a* god; he was always regarded as the manifestation in act of the one and only God. But so intimate, so decisive, so supreme had been that manifestation, and so all-embracing was the wholeness of life brought by his impact upon them, that in their conviction he came to be linked with God in a unity which was more intense than if he had only "showed" God without sharing in what he showed. Later this insight of Christian faith led to the application of such phrases as "God-Man" to Jesus Christ; unfortunate as language like that may have been, contradictory as it is to our ways of thinking, its intention is plain enough: true humanity and true Godhead are somehow brought together in the historical event wrought out in Jesus.

Once one has given up as incredible and impossible (save for mythological purposes) the Greek idea of a god who comes down to earth and walks about as a human being, there are two possibilities open for the interpretation of Jesus Christ. One is that human nature is nothing other than potential divinity, which *realizes* its potentiality in this person. If in Jesus we have perfect human nature, then by definition Jesus is also divine. That possibility seems to be ruled out for the theist, whose view of the relation between God and creation has been molded by the general biblical understanding of things. For Scripture—and I think for common sense—God and creation are not, and cannot become, identical. The world is *in* God, God is *in* the world. It is penetrated by God who works through it and can lure it to serve God's purposes, but God and the world are never the same reality, not even in human nature at its highest. The other possibility—and the one I believe makes much more sense and is more in accord with the biblical witness—is that in Jesus the energizing and indwelling activity of God in human creation reaches a climactic stage. To say this presupposes that in all men and women there is some working of deity, varying in degree and intensity, while those in whom there is a greater fullness of response to the divine working become more adequately the personal instruments for God. And that movement and activity can very well be clinched, so to speak, in Jesus, who would thus be (in von Hügel's words) "the implied goal and center" of all God-human mutuality and interrelationship. Therefore, what God did in Jesus would be an act of singular intensity with real speciality, but still in human terms and under human conditions. Response on the human side would be shown by increasing moral and spiritual discernment, obedience to the divine will, and dedication to the divine intention; but God would remain God and the personhood would remain entirely human. Human potentiality is not toward becoming divine, but toward so responding to the divine initiative that the Self-Expressive Activity of God would have what Athanasius styled an *organon*—a personal instrument open to employment by God but with full human freedom retained—adequate for the divine purpose. This would indeed be incarnation in a climactic sense.

It cannot be proven that this occurred in Jesus. As I said, to speak in such a way is part of our interpretation, by way of suggesting *how* God and humanity can effectively be brought together in an enduring unity of act. But although it cannot be demonstrated from the Gospel material, it may be believed; and belief in this instance would be supported by the response we ourselves make to what Jesus does for us by quickening in us the selfsame working of the Word in our own lives and by the deepening response we may then be enabled to make to that Word. In some such fashion we can come to understand the Christian conviction that through Jesus Christ God is decisively present and at work, "representing" (in Schubert Ogden's admirable word) the possibility present in human nature as such, establishing a reconciliation of human existence with God's intention for it, and revealing the divine nature in human terms and with a singular intensity.

In the developing Christian apprehension of the meaning of Jesus Christ, responsible and careful thinkers have never claimed that he is *absolutely* God, yet it has consistently been asserted that he is the one in whom God so energized—or "dwelt," in the Johannine phrase—as to make it right to call him the Incarnate Word of God. We today may prefer other ways of getting at the point, and that is our privilege. But if it is such we must remember always that our Christian ancestors were using what for them was the best available wording to express their, and our, deepest conviction when we are true to the continuing witness of experience of life in Christ.

Those ancient thinkers worked with the concept of the Logos, as we have seen. The Logos, or Word, was the expressive mode of the divine reality. The patristic age believed that in the mystery of Godhead this Word is always indwelling (*endiathetos*), eternally the movement of God from and in the divine self. In the creation of the world, they thought, the Word is outward-moving, the agent by whom all creation is effected (*prophorikos*). In every human life made in the image of God, however defaced by sin that image may be, the Word is present and active as the ground and linking of humanity with God (*spermatikos*). In Jesus Christ, in whom God's image emerges in grace and truth on the level of human existence, as such existence makes full response to God's prior initiating activity, the Word is "en-manned" (*enanthropesas*).

This, in brief, is what patristic Christology affirmed. In *The Word Incarnate* (Harper and Row, and Nisbet, 1959) I sought to give an account of this development and make sense out of it, but in a contemporary process idiom; and in *Christology Reconsidered* (SCM, 1970) I worked it over with a more extended and consistent use of that process conceptuality. I mention these two books simply because a reader may be interested in a further and more adequate discussion by the same author along the same lines.

Much official theology seems to have gone wrong, first, in confining the incarnating action of God to Jesus alone, so that he appears to enter the world as a catastrophic intrusion, as someone has put it, unrelated to the rest of the God-world and God-humankind relationship; and second, in speaking of Jesus in "substance" idiom, thus suggesting a static deity who in some fashion is implanted in, takes the place of, or is incomprehensibly united with another static "substance" called human. In a world which is dynamic through and through, however, we cannot speak of static substances but must talk of events or acts or happenings. Hence divine Action and human responsive action make more sense to us. This makes it possible, and right, to agree with Basil Willey, who once remarked that the human life of Jesus was so one with God, in will and intentionality, that in him the life of God was lived in a human being, by a human being, and for humanity. For us he is "adequate," as a modern saint has said. He provides us with a clue to the nature of God disclosed in the divine activity; he gives us a clue to our own humanity in its proper functioning; and he re-presents the right relationship between those two. The image of God is in Jesus emergent in full humanity. He is no outlandish anomaly but rather the classic instance of divine Activity in human expression.

This Christian conviction neither depends on nor demands belief in what is often called the virgin birth. Humanly speaking, we may believe, Jesus was the son of Joseph and Mary. The stories told in the first two chapters of Matthew and Luke are apologetic, or christological, in intent, and they cannot be taken as historical narratives. Insistence on a biological virgin birth has been a mistake, though an understandable one. But the results have been unfortunate in that they have suggested a low view of the sexual act, minimized the genuineness of Jesus' humanity, and entailed a distorted picture of the meaning of incarnation itself. The creedal phrases "conceived by the Holy Ghost, born of the Virgin Mary," are properly understood as a way of affirming the speciality of Jesus, not as a way of making his conception unnatural. The special pleadings of some theologians on this point, along with talk about the virgin birth as necessary because in Jesus the Word came *into* the world and not *out of* it, are convicted of absurdity on the face of it. The latter statement, especially, is really based on a deistic view of an absentee God who must "come into" a world which on any Christian, biblical, and theistic view God can never have left. Surely we should talk in terms of intensity of divine Activity and fullness of human response, not in terms of "above" and "below," "in" and "out," "entrance," and the like—these are mythological terms, and for our own day they are *outworn* rather than significantly evocative mythological terms.

Much the same may be said concerning the miracle stories in the Gospels. The point of these stories is not that they are veridical reports of what happened in Palestine in the first century; we can never hope to have any such "newspaper reportage" of the life, deeds, or even teaching of Jesus. Their importance lies in their relating to us the astounding impact upon men and women of Jesus' life and what he accomplished. Thus these stories have an implicit theological value in their testimony to the conviction of those who were Jesus' companions and of those who through the earliest preaching came to believe in him, that "no [person] ever spoke like this man," no person ever did the things this man did. We can neither rationalize the miracle stories in order to make them more credible nor accept them as if they were literal and scientific truth. But we *can* read them and use them as witness to the reality of the divine Activity in and through Christ, stated in terms and through stories that belong to a world of historical and scientific thought different from the world in which we live.

The great positive truth with which the Christian fellowship has insistently been concerned—and hence its central assertion or "gospel"—is that in Jesus Christ God has "visited and redeemed" creation. Even that is phrased in a poetic and symbolic way, but its point is clear. (Not that this Jesus is incarnate simply as a remedy for sin; we shall discuss this aspect of the matter in the following section.) Above all, what God has "determined, dared, and done" (to use Christopher Smart's grand words in *The Song of David*) in Jesus is to crown all previous incarnating and revelatory activity for the human race, thus re-presenting what God is always up to vis-à-vis humanity. Yet it is also the case, as the next section will seek to show, that to men and women who need a Lord whom they can adore, a "Pattern" (as Kierkegaard put it) they can follow, and a Savior who will bring them wholeness of life when they know and acknowledge their selfishness and sin, Christ is God's supreme Deed for us and for our salvation.

3. *He was crucified "for our sake."* The Christian affirmation that Jesus was crucified "for our sake" is often stated by the use of the word atonement, a word that will serve if we remember that etymologically it means "at-one-ment." Through the event we name when we say "Jesus Christ," and supremely through what happened on the cross on Calvary with all this implies, human existence is made "at one" with God.

Before we can begin to make sense of this kind of talk, however, we need to recognize that the human situation as we know it and share in it is marked by alienation and estrangement. Later, in our discussion of human nature, we shall have more to say about this. At this point it is sufficient to say that for the moment we recognize that we are not what we might be, that human existence is in defection from its proper fulfillment, and that we are in need of the wholeness of life which will put us on the right path and enable us to become more and more what God intends for us to be.

Unfortunately, many of the theologies that have sought to describe the process of at-one-ment have been so complicated—sometimes so sub-Christian—in their assumptions that they have obscured rather than helped to explicate the truth of the matter. Indeed, the truth of the matter can never be fully explained, for like all personal relationships in their depth and in their strange yet wonderful capacity to enrich our living—of human life with God's life, of men and women with each other—there is a mystery here which we must accept with "natural piety" but which we can never hope to explicate with utter clarity. If I can never adequately state the significance of my relationships with those whom I love in this world, or give a neat description of how I can overcome the alienation and estrangement of myself from another, or describe with any fullness what it means to be accepted by another and loved in spite of my deficiencies and my self-centeredness, I can never state in other than symbolic idiom the opening of further human possibilities with the overcoming of human deficiencies in my relationship with God— a relationship that has been broken by my wilfullness and sin.

Yet I can have intimations of what it is all about. And here it is possible to use (if this is done with care and understanding) what is said in the older theologies, as symbols of truths which must be safeguarded. They are certainly not exhaustive accounts of what "at-one-ment" means and how it is accomplished, but they do point to aspects that are significant. And they represent ways in which, under given conditions and in given circumstances, men and women have felt that they were "saved" from what dragged them down and damaged their lives, and that they were being drawn as they responded in commitment of self to the action of God in Jesus Christ. The various theories of atonement can be subsumed under two general heads: first, what God in Jesus does toward humanity; and second, what Jesus in his full humanity does toward God. As there is in Jesus divine Action and human response, so in the making of men and women to be at one with God and with their neighbors, there is action humanward and response Godward.

In the totality of Jesus' human life, obedient to the will of God even to the point of death, there is the enactment, on the stage of history and in the circumstances of human existence, of the right relationship of that existence with God. We are meant to be obedient children, but in fact we are children of disobedience. The old legend of the Garden of Eden portrays the way we seek to fulfill our own desires and in so doing deny our true nature. *De te fabula:* the story is the story of each one of us, exiled by false self-seeking from the garden of human obedience and hence from human happiness into the strange land where we seek only our own way and hence lose our intended happiness. But Jesus does what we should do but do not do: he lives in obedience to God. If we are joined with Jesus in a fellowship of surrendering love we too may be enabled to do through him what we are meant to do. The wonderful truth is that through such surrendering love, through willingness to unite ourselves with him, we are indeed joined with Christ and in him we can give ourselves in obedience to God.

But we can do this only because God has first sought us out. And that is the first point of "at-one-ment." Jesus is that one in whom God acts focally toward us, in loving revelation and manifestation, calling forth our response. When, in obedience to what he believed to be God's unmistakable will, Jesus went to the cross and died there so that God's sovereign rule might be visibly established (in New Testament language, that the kingdom of God might come), he demonstrated the love of God for humanity. Hence he became the sacrament of God's love; in him the Action of God, which is the love of God, was decisively at work. Here is the God-humanward side of the total reality, just as obedient surrender to God is the human-Godward side.

The interpretation of the atonement which makes most sense to me is a combination of Abelard's position, of God's exhibiting in act unfailing love for humanity, with what might be styled an ontological grounding, in the very structure and dynamic of the cosmos, for what was done in Christ. Abelard's position has been seriously misinterpreted, spoken of as "merely exemplarist." The fact is that Abelard was trying to say, with his own passionate awareness of what love can mean in human experience, that in Jesus, God gave us not so much an example of what we should be like but—and this is the big point in his teaching—a vivid and compelling demonstration in a concrete event in history that God does love humanity and will go to any lengths to win from them their glad and committed response. When this is combined with what I have called an "ontological" grounding—that such love in concrete act is precisely what God always is and how God always acts—we have a picture that is so overwhelmingly real, so profoundly effectual, that it makes things different. Or, better, it enables us to see that things *are* different from what we had thought to be the case; hence we are drawn to respond with a heart's surrender in answering love. This is no mere subjective view. It is objective, because it stresses *what God does;* and the subjective side is only our answer, perhaps our feeble answer, to that doing.

There have been many other theories of atonement, each picking out what a given generation took to be the worst possible human situation and going on to affirm that in the action of God in Jesus, God met us precisely at that point: slavery to demonic powers, from which we have been delivered; actual slavery to human masters, with manumission accomplished in Christ; guilt for wrongdoing, with Christ as the advocate who pleads for, and secures, our release; corruptibility and mortal death, met in Christ with healing and eternal life. . . . And so it goes, even including the medieval idea that no human penance can give God the honor due but that in Christ this has been provided and so men and women are released from their wrongdoing. None of these views should be taken as anything but a way in which the deeply felt experience of forgiveness and at-one-ment with God is known; they are "sociologically conditioned," as it would be phrased today. But they *do* point to an abiding reality known by those who have become able, thanks to God's working in Christ, to find freedom from a damaging past and to live toward an en-graced future.

On the cross, where Love went to the limit of death, we are shown for what we are in our sin—unloving, self-willed, in contrast to that Love. Our defects, our weakness, our failures to follow and to attain what we know to be right—all are now recognized for what they are: not harmless peccadilloes, but thoughts and words and deeds that tend to kill God who is active within us. We are sinners, which is to say, "we have done those things which we ought not to have done, and left undone those things which we ought to have done." We have broken the intended relationship which is ours with God. That does not mean, and should not ever be taken to mean, that we are utterly depraved in the sense that we are nothing more than a mass of corruption. Never is the image of God, toward which we are moving and which is the light of the *Logos spermatikos* in us ("the light that enlightens" every person, as John puts it) utterly and totally destroyed. The image is there, however terribly dimmed; the light is still in us, however feebly it is allowed to shine. We are estranged from the God who nonetheless never leaves us. It is in us, in our ways and our works, that the estrangement exists, not in God, who is deeper in us than our own selves, as Augustine, in a happier mood, rightly said in his *Confessions.*

But health is not *in us,* as we seek the lower levels of our own will and way; health or wholeness, the full well-being of our existence as God's children, is *in God;* it always was and always will be in God, who is the fountain of life and light and love. What we need is to be set on the path to that health. And this we find in Jesus: "Thou of life the fountain art, / Freely let me take of thee." So Wesley put it. And so every man or woman who has turned to Jesus has discovered. Through the act of God in the event of Jesus Christ, the fountain of life is opened and given to God's children to drink. So when we are turned from our wrong self-will to God manifest in the love wrought out in Christ, we are reconciled, made "at one" with God, made "at one" with our neighbors, made "at one" with ourselves. The split in our inner person is healed; we are made whole.

Not that this takes place instantaneously. It takes time. Once we are ready to accept the fact that we are accepted although we know very well that we are unacceptable, the process has begun. Paul Tillich took delight in stating it in that fashion, and he was surely right in doing so. Once we turn to God we are on our way home. But it is likely to be a long way, and we must be patient. To change the image, the "old Adam" (our wrong self-will and our wrong self-seeking) takes a long time to die, even though the "new Adam" (the self that we see in Christ and would fain be) is at work in us and grows ever stronger as we look to God and commit ourselves to God and the divine healing work. The worship, prayer, and life of the Christian fellowship have their meaning here. They provide, as it were, the training school, the proving ground, the home in which this conversion, or continuing in our turning to God self-manifest because active in Christ, may be accomplished by God in us.

But why then the cross? We do not know, but at least we can see that it is by love poured out in death that the secret self-giving of God is made plain. Over the centuries Christians have seized on the cross as their central symbol, not by accident but because Christian insight has understood that it is in the one who loved us and gave himself for us that the truth about God and humankind is spoken; and that this loving and giving were consummated on Calvary. The alchemy by which evil is made into good, hatred becomes love, wrong is overcome by right is there demonstrated. The heart of God as compassionate co-sufferer with humanity is there disclosed as nowhere else.

Yet the cross is not the end, for life is stronger than death, love is the conqueror of hate, and God is the vanquisher of the evil imaginations of sinful men and women. So we come to the resurrection, Christ's conquest of death and his life received into God and therefore made available to humankind for evermore.

4. *He rose from the dead.* Throughout the New Testament rings the conviction that Jesus is no dead Master but the living Lord. He did indeed die, but he is "alive for evermore." The New Testament as a whole vibrates with the confidence that Jesus, who had been crucified just outside Jerusalem, was not destroyed by death but was still alive, with a fullness and intensity greater even than in the days of his flesh. He could not be held by death, the first Christians declared; in some fashion he had risen from the dead— and his kingdom will be forevermore.

What gave rise to this conviction? How can we today understand and accept it? To these two questions we must now turn.

First, it is plain that the empty tomb was not the originating factor since careful critical study of the material found at the end of all four Gospels makes it clear that the stories about the empty tomb are more in the category of Christian apologetic—however honestly believed and taught at the time when the Gospels were compiled from earlier oral tradition—than in that of historical reporting. Some biblical scholars, like Dr. John A.T. Robinson, would disagree at this point; they are certain that the empty-tomb material belongs to the earliest strata of tradition. But the majority of such scholars would probably emphasize what are usually styled the resurrection appearances.

For this we must turn to 1 Corinthians 15, which is probably considerably earlier than any of the Gospels in their written form. In that chapter Paul gives an account of how Christ appeared to, or was seen by (the Greek word may be translated either way), first Peter, then the Twelve, and so on, until "last of all" he was "seen by," or "appeared to," Paul himself. Just what these appearances involved presents a problem. Certainly they seem to have been "veridical visions," as Dr. E.G. Selwyn phrased it years ago in a well-known essay in *Essays, Catholic and Critical,* not hallucinations or mere imagining in a fanciful sense. Whatever may have been the psychological process—and about this we can only speculate—the fact remains that these visions were inextricably associated with the earliest conviction that the Jesus who had died, who had been buried, who had seemed to be put out of the way had proved that he had conquered death, or, as the New Testament puts it, had been raised by God from death.

There have been many attempts to work out the details of the events that led to belief in the resurrection of Christ, even to reconcile the patently irreconcilable details of the stories about the empty tomb. The results are not very convincing. The material is so much in the category of imaginative discourse and so little in the category of strict or "scientific" history that this exercise seems futile. Yet something *does* remain: the unquestionable fact that the earliest stories testify to the disciples' firm certainty that God had vindicated Jesus' obedience unto death, that Jesus was therefore alive, and that they were in contact with him, not only as one whom they remembered but as one whose reality they could and did now experience.

We can say with complete confidence that this certainty turned discipleship to Jesus from a belief held by a small Jewish sect into faith in a living Lord who was *with God* and also *with God's people* here on earth. Such a conviction could not have sprung from mere hallucination or sheer illusion. In some fashion God assured the earliest believers that this Jesus who had been crucified by Jewish and Roman connivance was indeed both Lord and Christ. He had been vindicated in his obedience to what he took to be God's will; the love that had marked his earthly life could not be destroyed but was now secure forever in the divine life—and he was known to his people as a present reality.

But how can we today understand and accept this? That is

our second question. Here our process conceptuality can assist us. It will be recalled that this conceptuality insists that there is a mutuality between God and the world such that each influences and affects the other. Not only is the created order open to the divine action but the supreme reality we call God is also open to receive the action taken in the created world. Things that happen there have their effect upon God as God adapts the divine self to and employs that which occurs in the world. God remains always faithful to the divine nature and mode of activity, is always Love-in-action. Yet God's manner of relating the divine self to creation can be adjusted to what God has received from it; and God responds in appropriate ways to what has gone on there. Thus we may suggest that the total event of Jesus Christ, reaching its climax on the cross, is a matter not of the *dead* past but of the *living* past in the divine life. And in God's continuing relationship with humanity, that living past plays its central role in God's dealing with men and women. God is alive, and Christ is alive in God, in whatever mode or manner is appropriate to God's way of remembering and treasuring the achievements wrought out in creation and among men and women in their concrete existence.

Furthermore, this truth was communicated to the first believers by visions, or in some other fashion, so that they have a surety about it proper for their time and place. Thus the contemporary Christian is in one sense dependent upon and shares in the primitive Christian conviction. In another sense the Christian of today can also confirm that conviction in personal experience as a member of the Body of Christ, the Christian fellowship. This can happen because such discipleship brings newness of life here and now. As Jesus died, so the Christian dies to sin; as Jesus was raised from death, so the Christian rises to newness of life *in Christ*, letting the victorious love which was in Christ and which was released through him into the world, take possession of his or her existence.

Thus the resurrection of Christ is not merely an event in a past that is now over and done with but also a continuing event, first of all in God and then in people who have surrendered or committed themselves to Christ. The "resurrection life" is the life of those who are with Christ in their here-and-now existence. And those who live in Christ have what the Johannine writer called "eternal life" with him. The same writer has Jesus say, "This is eternal life, that they know thee the only true God, and Jesus Christ whom thou hast sent."

10

The Spirit and the Divine Triunity

The writer of a devotional book I read more than forty years ago—a book whose author and title I have forgotten—made an interesting point about the Holy Spirit. The writer described the Spirit, in a phrase I have *not* forgotten, as "the humblest person in the Godhead." That may not be a particularly happy phrase, but the idea the writer was seeking to express is important. One could put it in other words and say that the Holy Spirit is most frequently unrecognized because the Spirit usually works anonymously among us. The Spirit, as we shall show more fully when we come to discuss the triunitarian conception of God, is concerned primarily with *response* to the outgoing, revelatory, and redemptive action of God. Hence there is always the possibility that the Spirit with the Spirit's responding work, will be equated or identified with the medium through which the response is made, more especially in the human movement of response.

In the years since the book mentioned above was written, we have witnessed an enormous growth in what is today called "the charismatic movement" in the Christian world. What was formerly taken to be a peculiarity of "holiness" sects has become a reality in the mainline churches; indeed, it has been said that the fastest growing group in these churches is composed of adherents of just this charismatic position. I do not wish to attack people who are charismatics and who both claim to know and also quite obviously manifest the fruit of the Spirit in visible ways. At the same time, it must be pointed out that in one sense at least such visible Spirit-filled response is a novel feature in the Christian fellowship, however many expressions of it may have occurred here and there in the past. And for theological purposes the phenomenon can be subsumed under the more general and less visible working of the Spirit as this has been known and presented in the work of Christian thinkers.

Now, while humanity's movement toward conformity with God's will and purpose as revealed in Christ is in its deepest reality the operation of the Holy Spirit, we are quite right to speak of this as also *our* response. Of course it *is* our response, but as we shall see, it is ours through the subtle and persuasive working of the Spirit within us, never denying or disregarding human freedom and accountability. Only by recognizing this double truth can we both see the genuine part that humankind plays in the whole God-world relationship and avoid the error of claiming that of ourselves, with but the slightest aid from God, we can achieve our own fulfillment.

As we read the New Testament we are struck at once by the fact that the emergent Christian community was possessed by a spirit (and I use here the lower case *s* intentionally) which bound it into a unity of discipleship, of worship, and of responding love to the Action of God in Jesus Christ. So profound and real was this spirit, so much more powerful than anything humankind could establish, so highly personal in its impact, that the early church was convinced that here, in this enthusiasm of which its members were so conscious, was an operation of the Spirit of whom the prophets had spoken in the older Israel. That Spirit had now been "poured out on all flesh," and the Christian fellowship, knowing the power which worked through it, called itself the fellowship of the Holy Spirit. So gradually it came to be understood that wherever and whenever human response is made to what is seen and known of the activity of God in the Word or divine Self-Expression, and in whatever manner or form, the basic significance of this response was to be found in the working of the Spirit of God within and among them. Or, as we might put it, spirit with a lower case *s* was tied in with and taken to be an operation of Spirit with an upper case *S*.

As with the development of the "doctrine of Christ," this is not the place to present a detailed account of the way in which the "doctrine of the Spirit" was discussed, stated, and finally more or less formalized in succeeding centuries. Our concern here is with the question of the meaning or significance of belief in the Holy Spirit for us today, using a process perspective to illuminate and help explicate the matter.

First of all, then, the work of the Holy Spirit is not to be confined to the Christian fellowship, although there have been some theologians—and great ones at that—who have been guilty of such parochialism in their thinking about the Spirit. The common sense of the Christian ages, however, has been much more generous in its understanding. It has been impelled to say that just as the eternal Word of God— God in God's Self-Expression worldward—is not confined humanly speaking to Jesus Christ but rather *defined* in him, so also the activity of the responding Spirit of God is defined but not confined to the specifically Christian response in faith within the Christian community. The danger of seeing the Holy Spirit simply in the context of Christian life—and, even worse, solely in the context of ecclesiastical experience —is that we narrow intolerably one great aspect of the operation of God in the world. This is both absurd and blasphemous.

We ought to be willing to acknowledge that when an artist, for example, responds with his or her whole being to the aspect of reality that has been disclosed and seeks to set down on canvas that truth, it is at bottom the Holy Spirit who is enabling and empowering the artist. So also the poet is often compelled to say the work he or she has done was his or her own, yet (in a phrase of D.H. Lawrence's) "the wind that bloweth through me" has been in and behind that work. The sense of being possessed, of being grasped and used by something not ourselves but through which we realize our fullest potentialities, is indeed familiar to us all, although not necessarily in the vivid and striking way a person of genius or a great saint can know it. The honest effort to do one's duty, the attempt to live one's life in love and charity with others, the deep concern for justice for the underprivileged, the pursuit of goodness, or the search for truth, and all else that conforms our lives to the pattern of their intended perfection can only be explained when we have seen that in the last resort there is a working of the Spirit of God in each of these human situations.

We may say also that the same principle applies in the natural world. The growth of the acorn into the oak is, from one point of view, the unfolding of latent potentialities that are describable in scientific terms, just as the process of "conversion," from false centering on the self to releasing openness to God, is describable in psychological or sociological terms. Yet at bottom the growth into the pattern of oakhood that is intended for the acorn is given proper theistic meaning only when we can say that deeper than any scientific description, and in no sense contradicting that description, the divine drive to fulfillment of potentiality has been at work. So also with conversion. The Christian doctrine of the triunitarian nature of God, to which we shall come in the latter part of this chapter, is a symbolic account that gives a better ultimate explanation of what the *whole* story is about than does some account true (so far as it goes) which is given in scientific (or similar) terms alone.

The intensity, although not always the *recognizable* intensity, of the working of the Spirit is in proportion to the intensity (again not always recognizable) of the divine Action to which it is a response. That is why in the fellowship of Christians the Spirit is believed to be more adequately known and more fully at work than elsewhere. Above all, that is why in Jesus himself—who (as we argued in the preceding chapter) is best conceived as that human existence where the divine Action was incarnate, given adequate expression, in human life—it could be said that "it is not by measure that [God] gives the Spirit." In Jesus there is both the focus of the divine Action, the eternal Word or divine Self-Expression, in created things and also the focus of the divine Response (which we may now capitalize), the Holy Spirit who moves graciously in creation to lure it on toward its proper end.

Furthermore, in each of us it is the Spirit who works in us gently and quietly for the most part but also sometimes powerfully and overwhelmingly, molding us to Christ. This is the basic meaning of the theological term "sanctification." We are being made holy—that is, being made to belong more and more to God and to reflect more and more God's character of love, goodness, righteousness, truth—as the Holy Spirit works within our human wills and lives. It is the same Spirit too who by divine "inward testimony" (as the Reformers of the sixteenth century phrased it) or deeply experienced witness enables us to recognize that same divine Action, in lesser degree and in different fashion to be sure, but nonetheless truly, wherever God is moving toward us, soliciting an answer from us, awakening desire in us, urging us to respond to the divine revelatory act.

The Christian is bound to believe that in its growing apprehension of the significance of Jesus, the church was led by the Spirit who informs it to discern more and more of the meaning of the Man of Nazareth. The historian might see but the best of all people, the great Jewish prophet who crowned a long series of prophets of the older Israel. The Spirit-informed faith of the Christian community, by that Spirit's deepening the insight of all men and women, brought about the understanding of Jesus as more than a prophet, more even than the best of all people. That Spirit-informed faith came finally to see in Jesus the one in whom God dwelt or through whom God worked with singular intensity, to provide a re-presentation of what God is always up to in the world and intends for humanity. Thus it may rightly be said that the Spirit guides the Christian fellowship "into all truth," "taking of the things of Christ and declaring them unto us." It may seem that to emphasize the pervasive operation of the Holy Spirit, as well as to stress the Spirit's focal action in the life of Jesus and its consequences, will in the end reduce men and women to mere automatons used by God with no respect for their freedom, their dignity, and their own responsible decisions, without any personal or social human contribution to the process. But the fact is that in human existence our highest freedom is found not in our self-will or our attempts to be on our own but in the opening of that existence to the divine reality. "Our wills are ours, to make them thine," wrote Tennyson. "In God's will is our peace," said Dante. And Augustine said, "Thou hast made us toward thee; and restless is our heart until it finds rest in thee."

But how can we understand this? I believe that the mystery of human love will help us here. We know that it is not when we are self-centered and concerned only with doing what we please that we find our deepest happiness and realize our best human fulfillment. We find these when we lovingly surrender ourselves to those for whom we care. We must indeed do our part; we are in that sense free to choose, free to decide, free to act in this way or that. But being in love is always a matter of grace; it is a gift much more than it is an achievement entirely our own. We never say, if we think about it carefully, that self-surrender in love is nothing more than a work we do or something we accomplish by ourselves. Nothing is so pathetic or so frustrating as the attempt to *buy* love or *earn* it. Such attempts come to a dead end. Love can only be *received*, as we are caught up into the surrender of self to self. In that experience we remain ourselves, in all our personal identity and with all our freedom and responsibility; yet we are mysteriously and wonderfully "oned" with another, so that the other person lives in us and we in him or her.

I used this analogy earlier in my attempt to get at the significance of Jesus as what has traditionally been called the incarnation of God in human existence. But the same analogy may be used as an aid to understanding the working of the Holy Spirit within us. We do indeed respond, since we as humans have that capacity. Yet in the depths of our being, the Spirit responds in us and through us. This is an example of what theologians have styled "synergism"—a working together in which *we* act but in which the Spirit *also* acts. And the Spirit's act, like all divine action, is "prevenient"—prior and preparatory—to our human response. Thus we can assert that our highest and finest moments are indeed ours and yet also reflections of, expressions of, movements of, the action of the Spirit who works with us as Paul puts it, "bearing witness with our spirit that we are children of God." I believe that once again process thinking helps us to reach this conclusion.

Christian thinkers in the West have spoken regularly of the Spirit of the Father *and the Son*. In the East, however, the words I have italicized have never been used, although thinkers in the Eastern church have agreed that one might say "the Father *through the Son*." This may seem a petty theological quarrel, but it is not. As we shall see, an important truth is at stake, although to understand it we need to consider the triunitarian nature of God.

In the development of Christian thought it has been stressed that the Spirit of God, while indeed the Spirit come from God the Father, is the Spirit who is mediated to the world through the Son. However, this ought not to be taken to mean that it is through Jesus only that the Spirit comes. The word Son here refers to the eternal Word of God, the divine Self-Expression, who in much Christian discourse has been called "the Son"—although some of us regret this because it tends to confuse things when a term appropriate to Jesus as humanly God's Son is applied to the divine reality itself. Something about this will be said later in this chapter. For the present, however, the point is that the quality of the Spirit, and hence our criterion for knowing whether any given spirit is indeed to be linked with the Spirit of God, is for Christians the congruity which that spirit does, or does not, possess with what we have learned of God, God's character and purpose and manner of operation, through Jesus Christ in his revelation of the divine nature and agency in the world.

In other words, we need to determine whether the spirits are of God or whether they are misleading and alien. The way to test them is to determine whether or not they point to and are consistent with what we know of God's love, God's goodness, God's righteousness, and God's saving power in Jesus. Thus all that is upbuilding, expressive of love and tenderness, eager for the right, concerned for justice, informed by courage, able to establish sound relationships and sound dealings—all that manifests beauty and that speaks of truth—all this is the working of God, who moves in the world by the Word and from that world receives the Amen of responsive conformity through the Holy Spirit active in the creation.

It was in the attempt to state these profound truths that thinkers within the Christian fellowship, building upon what has been called "the Palestinian experience of God," came to develop the distinctively Christian conception of God: God as "triune," God as the unity of three interpenetrating modes of activity. In an earlier day, when a "substance" philosophy was prevalent, this was talked about as "the divine subsistence," not only as if God were to be distinguished from the world but also as if God's existence was somehow other than God's activity. Such a view cannot be maintained when we come to see that "a thing *is* what it *does*" (in words of Whitehead already quoted) and when we have to do not with substances but with events or occasions or (again to quote Whitehead) "actual entities" which are essentially "becomings" rather than "beings." With this reminder we may now turn to a consideration of the doctrine of the divine Triunity—and notice that I have said "triunity" rather than "trinity," because the latter carries a suggestion only of *three* divine realities, whereas the former makes it more obvious that our discussion is about some "three *in one*" and thus preserves the essential unity or oneness of God from the possibility of slipping away into polytheism.

There is an ancient Christian theological document miscalled "the Athanasian Creed" (it had nothing to do with Athanasius himself but was evidently the work of Hilary of Poitier and should be given its proper name of *Quicumque Vult*) that can help us here. Whatever fault we may find with that document in other respects—and Anglicans may be grateful that it is no longer commonly said, as ancient prayer books required, at public worship on certain great festivals of the Christian year—it gives us the right understanding of this triunitarian conception of God when it affirms "This is the Catholic faith: that we *worship* Godhead in Trinity, and Trinity in Unity." Outlandish and absurd as this may sound to the non-Christian, it puts the emphasis just where it belongs. The faith in God is supremely acted out in worship; and for a Christian loyal to the Christian community that worship is of "God *the Father*," manifested in what through *the Self-Expression* (and for us supremely in the event of Jesus Christ) God has done, is doing, and will do in the creation, and given response through the working of *the Holy Spirit*, enabling the world and humans within it to say their Amen to God's initiating activity.

If this doctrine of the triunity of God were merely intellectual speculation or an intellectual answer to an intellectual problem, it might be interesting to academic minds; it might be a way of meeting a difficult question and providing a better or worse solution to that question. But it would not be much more than that. And some recent attempts to do away with the conception have been at that level. The trouble is that they have taken the doctrine of the divine Triunity to be a literal statement about God. But it is much more a symbolic kind of speaking about the ways in which God's human children have come to think about deity, in the manner of their worship and prayer, quite as much as in their attempts at faithful discipleship. Process thinking will help us see that God and the world are in mutual relationship. Its talk about God as primordial and as the continuum of all possibility, about God as consequent—affected and influenced by the creation—and about God as "superjective" in giving back to creation the transfigured and enriched contributions it has made to the deity, may suggest certain parallels to the traditional doctrine, although to work in this fashion is both unnecessary and misleading. We do better to follow the suggestion of Prof. Hartshorne who on one occasion remarked to me that this doctrine, like the traditional ones of incarnation and atonement, should be seen as valued, historically-freighted symbols that provide insight into God and God's ways in the creation. And precisely because we "*worship* Godhead in Trinity, and Trinity in Unity" we can see the appropriateness of just such symbolism. For worship, above all, is imaginative, poetical, or metaphorical; and its language should never be taken as if it were as exact as, say, would be an entomologist's description of markings on some insect's back! Triunitarianism is a matter of "high religion" not of logical discourse.

It is not too difficult to see how the belief in God as "Trinity in Unity"—Triune God—came to develop. First of all, there was the God of Israel, whom the early Christians, like their Jewish neighbors, believed to be the one and only God of the whole earth. In "advanced" Judaism this God was identified with the "supreme God" of other religions, although there were special characteristics such as divine righteousness and loving-mercy (*chesed*) found in the Jewish picture more than in some of the others. Jewish thought was thoroughly monotheistic, at least from the time of Second Isaiah if not before. But although the God of Israel was identified with the one God of all monotheistic religions, divine self-revelation through the history and experience of the Jewish people had given this God, as we have just noted, a special quality. This God was indeed creator and sovereign ruler, but also the God who would and did communicate the divine self to humankind, so that they could know God as the loving parent of those children.

And then came Jesus. He lived as a man with other men and women. He was known and loved, followed as master and revered as teacher. He believed that he was sent from God with a mission in the world. In the end, that mission included his death on the cross. But afterward, by what have been called "many infallible signs," the members of the early Christian community were convinced that he was not a figure in the dead past but was somehow wonderfully alive as their present, living, and active Lord. They found it natural and proper to try to relate him to God who had sent him. At first they saw him as Messiah, the supreme representative of God come to establish God's kingdom in the world. But soon they felt that this was not sufficient.

What Jesus had been and continued to be for them, what he had done and continued to do, were so tremendous in their impact on those who responded to him that they found themselves compelled to say that in Jesus God had "visited and redeemed" humankind. Using ideas which, as we have seen, were derived from both Jewish and Greek thought, they spoke of him as the Word of God made flesh—or, as we have preferred to say, that One in whom the divine Action so possessed and used a human life that here God's Self-Expression was seen focally in a genuine and complete human existence. So there was not only the God of Israel but also Christ the Lord, the "tabernacling" of God with us in a supreme action for human wholeness.

Nor was that all. For as we have been saying, the early Christians knew themselves to be united in a community of loving, worshiping, and obedient response to the Action of God in Christ; and that community, in their experience, was no ordinary social grouping but itself a working of God among them and within them. It was, they believed, the Holy Spirit who created that community, moved through it, worked in it, and urged its members toward conformity with the pattern given in Christ by God. Whatever we may think about this, whatever revisions we may wish to make in its statement, the fact remains that it was in the fellowship of the Spirit that the God of Israel was freshly experienced as "the God and Father of our Lord Jesus Christ." In the New Testament this is not worked out in any detail. Maybe it would have been better to leave it—as it was at the start—a matter of a threefold experience which for such strict monotheists as the early Christians could only be explained as somehow integral to, yet distinctive within, the reality of God in the divine fullness. Paul puts the experience in well-known words when he writes of "the grace of the Lord Jesus Christ and the love of God and the fellowship of the Holy Spirit," certainly an incipient triunitarian formula but yet stated in the idiom of religious life.

Thus the doctrine of the divine Triunity developed first in very simple terms, then more in the form in which it has become part of the theological tradition of the Christian community. One of the most difficult problems associated with this development was the safeguarding of the genuine divinity of the Action of God in Jesus Christ and of the Response (Response, with an upper case R, since we are talking about a truly divine operation) in the Holy Spirit. Certainly for devotional purposes it is hard if not impossible to distinguish between these two; indeed, it is equally difficult to distinguish these two from whatever is known of "God the Father." Professor Geoffrey Lampe has remarked (and I believe what he says is correct) that

> those who talk of meeting and speaking to Jesus would find it hard to explain the difference between that experience and encountering, or being encountered by, God: and in fact I think the latter is what they actually mean: they are experiencing God who was in Jesus, God who is, therefore, recognized by reference to the revelatory experience recorded in the New Testament and reflected upon in the whole subsequent Christian tradition. (*God as Spirit*, Oxford University Press, 1977, p. 21.)

Certainly we need to make sure that we do not talk as if there were three gods. It was for the early Christians and for later Christian reflection impossible to think that. The threeness represented more than transitory aspects of the divine reality, however, for God *is* Truth and surely God must let the divine self be known. After much trial and error, not to speak of a good deal of somewhat unseemly controversy, it was generally agreed that the divine Action in Christ was not to be restricted to Jesus alone, although in him it found what I have styled a "focus"; rather, that Action worldward is present and at work everywhere. So also with the Holy Spirit. The Spirit was active in, but not *only* in, the Christian life of response to God in Christ. In each instance, the specifically *Christian* reality was a manifestation of God in act, set in the context of a wider manifestation of God in act in all human experience, in all history, and in the whole natural order. Of that wider manifestation in act, what had taken place in Jesus and what took place in the Christian response was a vivid "re-presentation" of the whole range of divine operation.

We might phrase it in this way: In the event of Christ there is a concentration, as it were, of what goes on generally; in the response to Christ in Holy Spirit there is similarly a concentration of what goes on everywhere. The threefoldness of what might be named "the Palestinian Trinity" of early Christian days is a reflection of a cosmic triunity. But as I urged above, it would be wrong (in my judgment) to try to interpret all this too literally and logically; Prof. Hartshorne was right, I said, in saying that the symbol of the divine Triunity, like the "incarnation" and "atonement" as symbols, is much more appropriately retained *as a symbol*, as imaginative proclamation; it can then retain its indicative and suggestive value without our seeking to phrase it in the idiom of some particular philosophy or world view. In other words, the divine Triunity is a religious rather than a logically explicit affirmation. But this means that we are not to think that a word such as "persons," applied to Father, Word, and Spirit, can be interpreted in the way in which we today would use that term. In any event, even in the theology of the church the Greek word *hypostasis* (translated into the Latin as *persona* and then into the English as "person") had nothing like our modern sense. The Cappadocian fathers in the early church meant by that Greek word "abiding modes of being and activity"; Thomas Aquinas spoke in the Middle Ages of the "persons" of the Triunity as "relations in Godhead." I doubt if we need to worry ourselves about such technicalities, however, and if the suggestion I have quoted from Prof. Hartshorne is adopted, we have every reason to avoid any such worry.

The Christian conception of God in a triunitarian fashion has one value that must not be overlooked. It gives us a richer view than one which talks of deity as simply monadlike could do. Somehow in God the basic truth of personality is combined with the equally basic truth of sociality—and this has implications for our view of human nature, too, as we shall see in the next chapter. The triunity of God can serve as a symbol offering a hint or intimation into the mystery of God as God is active in the world; and our process conceptuality has made it clear that God *is* the divine Activity. To repeat Whitehead's saying, "A thing *is* what it *does.*"

I conclude with another important point. It has been conventional in philosophy of religion to talk of God as transcendent and as immanent. But there is possible a third term, not commonly found in such conventional discussion: "concomitance." The triunitarian picture intimates that God's activity in creation, and hence God in the depths of the divine nature, is both inexhaustible and unexhausted, and therefore that God is indeed transcendent. It intimates that God is "in" the creation, luring it to response and self-fulfillment, and therefore that God is immanent. But it also intimates that God is (as I like to put it) also "alongside" or "with" the creation, acting not only upon it and within it but also as self-identified with each and every created event or occasion. This may seem a highly speculative proposition, yet I am sure it has practical consequences, for it protects and values the variety of religious life. It makes a place for the sort of deism that when taken in separation from other ideas, tended to make God remote but also managed to assert the divine creatorhood and the divine transcendence. It makes a place also for the truth so imperfectly expressed in monism or a quasi-pantheistic notion of God as genuinely within things. And it also makes a place for a religiously minded "humanism," such as that found in some words of the ancient Christian writer Tertullian when he said, "When you see your brother, you see your Lord." Each of these, taken by itself, can lead to partial and even erroneous exaggeration, but when the three are combined it may very well be that a more adequate picture of God is set forth.

Nonetheless, the talk about the triune God began in a religious experience and is most adequately known in religious worship. The former—religious experience—need not be highly articulated nor even highly conscious of God *as God;* it may be vague, diffused, and unformed, yet also a deliverance of what it feels like to be dependent upon a reality greater than anything human or natural. The worship may not be explicitly developed in a trinitarian direction, but it does provide an opportunity to adore God in *all* God's ways and acts. Thus this conception of God can be *lived.* For any loyal Christian the worship of God as manifested in action in Christ, and the energizing of the Holy Spirit as an empowering for Christian living toward the image of God which in Jesus Christ is humanly visible, may very well be summed up in the versicle and response familiar to many in the "Catholic" churches:

> *Versicle:* Let us bless the Father and the Son with the Holy Spirit:
> *Response:* Let us praise and exalt *him* for ever.

I have italicized the pronoun him because it makes clear that no matter what we say about "threeness," we are committed also, and preeminently, to the "oneness" or unity of the basic thrust and drive in things we call "God."

11

The Person in Society

There is much talk nowadays about what we might call the nature of human nature. Some speak of human beings as essentially economic animals, others define them in terms of their sexual impulses, still others say that they are religious creatures. They have even been described, as I think Thomas Aquinas once suggests, as the animals who laugh. And of course there are the traditional ways of speaking about human nature; in the classical definition, to be human is to be "an animal substance with a rational nature."

Probably most of these ways of describing human nature are true so far as they go, or at least they contain elements of truth. But it seems to me that they are very partial and inadequate to the reality of what it feels like, to each of us, to *be* human. Certainly we are victims in one way or another of what are styled economic laws, say of supply and demand; surely we are in one aspect animals who seek for and require animal fulfillment; without a doubt we are sexual creatures. On the other hand, we can deal firmly with those so-called economic laws, while our animality is qualified by some degree of rational capacity and our sexual drive is far more than mere gratification of lust. So it goes, with most of the proposed definitions.

My own suggestion is simply that we recognize the truth

in much of what is said in these definitions and what is known about ourselves through the various sciences of our day, but that we refuse to confine our self-understanding to any one of them. Incidentally, for those of us who are concerned with matters of religion and faith, it is important that we avoid what may be for us a desirable, but is instead a dangerously partial, notion: that men and women are essentially "spiritual" beings. They *are* that, of course, but they are much else too, and I suspect that one of the reasons for the revolt against religion is that too often religiously minded people, lay or ordained, have talked of humankind in altogether too "spiritual" a fashion, forgetting so much else that is true of every person who has ever lived.

What then can a Christian say about human nature? And what can be said if that Christian also subscribes to the general process conceptuality presented and defended in this book?

I shall here set down my suggestions on this subject, putting them under separate headings, each with a Christian statement concerning it. After that, something will be said about these. The eight points to which I call attention are: (1) Human existence is a dependent one; in Christian language, "It is [God] who hath made us, and not we ourselves." (2) Human existence is an unfulfilled existence, with potentialities that may be realized or made actual; in Christian language, "God has made us toward himself." (3) Human existence is social in nature; in Christian language, "We are members one of another." (4) Humans are neither soul alone, nor mind alone, nor body alone, but organisms compounded of soul-mind-body; in Christian language, "We are made of the dust of the earth and that dust has had breathed into it the life which is given by God." (5) We are sexual creatures, in a much deeper sense than other creatures; in Christian language, "Male and female created [God] them" and "Human existence is a seeking of intimate relationships with others." (6) Humanity is sadly in defection from its deepest intentionality and unable to achieve proper fulfillment; in Christian language, "We are sinners." (7) We can be given wholeness of life, rightly integrated and thus fulfilled; in Christian language, we may be enabled "both to perceive and know what things we ought to do, and also may have grace and power faithfully to fulfill the same." (8) Nobody can be totally fulfilled without reference to God, in whose reception and employment of humanity our destiny is achieved; in Christian language, "We are restless until we find our rest in God."

Something like this, I believe, sums up the Christian view of human nature. But one further affirmation is required if we take seriously both our own inner self-awareness and the process way of interpreting it. Each of us also possesses some measure of genuine freedom, with its corollary of some measure of responsibility or accountability for our decisions made in that freedom. Our human existence can therefore be described in Berdyaev's phrase "creaturely freedom"; without that and apart from that, disregarding its central importance in our lives, we are given less than a complete picture. It is a merit of modern existentialist thinkers, including nontheists like Martin Heidegger and Jean-Paul Sartre, that they understand and insist upon this truth about human nature.

We may now turn to the first of our affirmations: We are dependent. We do not explain ourselves, we cannot keep ourselves in existence, we require that which is not ourselves in order to become ourselves. *Nobody* is entirely independent. Everybody is a *creature*, a created entity. It is most unfortunate that many people who would accept this fact in a general way find themselves unable to accept it in its specifically Christian phrasing, because it is still associated in their minds with the literal acceptance of the story of human creation told in Genesis in the Bible. One of our important duties, as I see it, is to be much clearer and much louder in our insistence that the Genesis story is myth and that no conclusions are to be drawn from it that presuppose its historical factuality. Once we are delivered from that error we can understand that the Christian assertion is that we depend not so much on some presumed first cause in the remote past but always and everywhere upon the creative and sustaining power of the basic reality working in and through the whole creation. Further, it should be said plainly that we are also constantly dependent upon more proximate realities, all of which are surrogates for our ultimate dependence. Family, friends, food, shelter, and the like; history, the accumulated knowledge and wisdom of the human race, nature and its products—these stand for and serve as instrumental agencies of the supreme reality which is the final dependability, the enduring strength of all creation, the chief creative cause and the chief receptive end in the cosmos. To pretend that we are independent is stupid; it is also vainglorious nonsense. As Ezra Pound wrote in *Pisan Cantos*, "Put down thy vanity . . . it was not *man* made grace or nature." A claim to human independence is in a way the root of our troubles; in the language of traditional moral theology it is the pride (*superbia*) which is the root sin of humankind. Baron Friedrich von Hügel, the great lay leader of Roman Catholic modernism in the early years of this century, spoke often of the need for "a humble sense of creatureliness." He was right; this awareness of our created dependence is for the Christian the motif that qualifies all one's thinking and doing. But it does not for a moment negate our creaturely freedom, to which we have made reference, nor does it minimize human dignity and responsibility for what is done in the world.

But we must go on to the second affirmation. We are unfulfilled existence. Each of us is an "unfulfilled capacity," made with and for a purpose—or, as our process conceptuality requires us to put it, "being made. . . ." The Christian would say that we are thus being made toward the image of God, to reflect, and personally (and socially) act for, the divine Love; and the deepest intentionality in us is in the direction of finding genuine fulfillment in fellowship with God. *Tu fecisti nos ad te, domine, et inquietum cor nostrum donec requiescat in te*—so Augustine said, in words I quoted in English earlier. I have given the Latin here because I wish to correct the usual and mistaken translation so often found, which makes Augustine say we are made *"for* God." Surely what he meant, and what the Latin with its *ad te* indicates, is that we are being made *toward* God, the force of the *ad te* in Latin being direction or end aimed at or desired. So we can say that human existence is being created, to push on toward the fulfillment of capacity possible only (in any ultimate sense) in communion and fellowship with God who alone can bring to flower the potentiality given in creation. But this brings with it the recognition that there are created surrogates as agents or means through which this may be done. It is when such surrogates are set up as *substitutes* or ends in themselves that they become demonic in their effect and distort the life of the one who rests in them. Any good reality, less than God, can serve as a means toward God. It is, alas, equally true that any such reality, put in the place of God, can pervert human life and bring it to tragic loss. Even religion can do this; and of that there have been plenty of instances in human history. It was Frederick Denison Maurice, the great English theologian of the nineteenth century, who warned that when people "cry out for the living God" it is all too easy to offer them "religion" instead. To substitute religion, granted all that is good and important in it, for God is always a temptation within the life of the ongoing Christian community.

Augustine spoke of the human heart as *inquietum,* "disquieted," until that heart "finds its rest in God." *Inquietum* is a very good word here. It expresses in Latin what is true in the claim of modern existentialists that *angst,* or "anxiety," as Kierkegaard put it, is part of the very existence of men and women in their alienation from the basic reality of their deepest selves. Why is this? I take it to be explained by the fact that our nature is dynamic, toward goals and toward fulfillment; we are creatures like that, yet we are unable in and of ourselves to achieve those goals. But unless we are moving in that direction, feebly and defectively as this will be, we are not genuinely human but only sophisticated simians. On the other hand, unless that movement is ultimately toward God, our restlessness reflects our serious and sometimes terrifying falling-short of that for which we exist. Ersatz fulfillment turns into dust and ashes.

Francis Thompson's poem "The Hound of Heaven" is often dismissed nowadays as a piece of flamboyant and exotic writing, but there have been few more eloquent expressions of the truth that "naught satisfieth" men and women which does not lead them to their true fulfillment in God. But once again we need to be careful lest we seem to insist that such fulfillment necessarily involves the acceptance of conventional patterns of theology or religious notions. One does not need to call the reality which thus fulfills human life by the *name* "God," although that is the hallowed way of pointing it out. An authentic Christianity will be glad to recognize God's incognitos, whatever they may be, wherever they may be; it will claim only that whatever tends to bring true fulfillment, integrating humans through some overmastering concern that grasps them, is the work of God; such "whatevers" are places and points where the divine action is known and something of the divine nature is made transparent to us, however we may name it. God, we must say, is not "jealous" in refusing to use surrogates that will have meaning for humanity.

I wish now to link the first two points with the Christian conviction that we are being made toward the image of God. The phrase "the image of God" means more than mere reflection as in a mirror; it means the active and energizing capacity given to humans, as created entities, to live with integrity as the "created second" of the God who is making them. At the heart of Christian faith is the figure of Jesus Christ as "the Express Image" of God. In him humanity is truly fulfilled. And it is not so much imitation of the picture of Jesus given in the New Testament as it is imitation of the response which is God's action and to which the New Testament witnesses, whereby God's intention in creating us "toward the divine self" is manifested in a concrete human life. Jesus is "what God is up to" with respect to human existence. It has been said that Jesus, in the totality of his life and deed, is "*God's* idea of humanity" visibly enacted before our eyes.

In our interpretation we have said that the most satisfactory way of understanding Jesus' significance is to see that in him there is made actual, real, vivid, and clear what is potential although unrealized or very partially realized in the rest of us. *His* response to the divine intention was adequate and complete, even if this cannot be demonstrated from the material in the Gospel narratives. But even in Jesus this achievement is not of and by a human being alone. God comes first; God always comes first. Thus Christian faith dares to say that here is not only a human deed—although of course it *is* that—but also, and here first, God's deed humanly speaking. God so energized through this particular human life, which had been divinely purposed and intended, that those upon whom it made and continues to make its impact have been obliged to say that in this man Jesus, God lived and wrought. And we should wish to claim that in Christ this is done as nowhere else, and never before so fully. So, once again God's focal presence and action in the man Jesus is incorrectly interpreted when it is taken to be primarily a rescue operation or an expedition into the world to bring humans back from their appalling situation of alienation and estrangement. It does indeed accomplish this, and therefore Jesus is rightly said to be our Savior. But in the first instance, and central to God's plan for humanity, it is the coronation (and the correction too) of God's continuing and consistent activity to bring about the fulfillment in us of the divine intention with which we are created.

In the third place, human existence is social. We are persons in society, living in commonality with our brothers and sisters. I need not dwell upon this fact since today it is so widely recognized and emphasized. We are all bound together in "a bundle of the living," as an Old Testament text says. More and more we are coming to grasp the validity of W.H. Auden's line "We must love one another or die." This Christian stress on sociality, which (as we shall see in

147

the next chapter) is the natural reason for the existence of the Christian community as well as of other human groupings, has a close relationship with the fourth assertion: that each of us is an organic unity, body-mind-spirit. Here recent developments in medical science, such as those in psychology, are offering invaluable confirmatory evidence of the biblical and Christian picture. We are not animals only, although we have animality in us. We are not angels, either, although we can think, aspire, value, love, and worship. Gabriel Marcel has protested against the saying "I have a body" and has insisted that in a profound sense it is much more true to say, "I am a body"—although that is not *all* I am.

To talk about ourselves as souls who happen to possess bodies is to make a grave mistake. Our identity is not found in some supposed substantial soul, as many theologians of the past have claimed; that identity is given in and through the series of concrete experiences which are ours from the past, in the present, and toward the future. What each of us is and does in bodily existence largely determines what we are. At the same time, we must recognize the significance of our spirituality, even when we reject spiritualism. (I am referring here not to the cult that goes by that name but to excessive emphasis on the nonmaterial in human life.) Once again a task is required from Christian teachers and preachers, both in what they have to say about human life in general and in what they have to say about Jesus in particular. Furthermore, this plain truth that we are organic psychosomatic "becomings" provides a natural reason for the use of sacramental means of worship and Christian nurture, as well as a vindication of the traditional emphasis on the eucharist or Holy Communion as central in our relationship, as Christian people, with the divine reality in whom alone we can find genuine fulfillment of our creaturely potentiality.

Related to this stress on the embodiment that is ours is human sexuality. Here is our fifth point. I remember well that on one occasion, speaking at a student conference, I said, "We are sexual beings." An undergraduate retorted in an audible voice, "Well, so are apes and apples." Of course apes and apples are sexual, but human existence is sexual in a different way from apes and apples. Of course there is a continuity between human sexuality and simian sexuality (about apples I cannot speak!), but at the human level sexuality is much more than a biological drive for the propagation of the species, accompanied as it is by pleasant feeling-tones that make it attractive to engage in sexual contacts. Human sexuality is intimately related to, indeed may be called the ground for, the drive toward self-fulfillment in a societal fashion. The biological instinct, which is real enough, is in men and women taken up into the yearning for relationship with other human beings; it is given a new significance and a new direction. It is much more a reflection of an urge toward unity with others than it is a reproductive urge, although the latter is often present.

Our sexuality is linked with our psychosomatic existence. In the human dynamic movement the body as well as the mind and spirit is present and active. We are so made that our chemistry, biology, and psychology, quite as much as our spirituality, are part of us. At the animal level there is an urge toward bodily union; at the emotional level there is an urge toward association with others of our kind, as intimately as possible. We are being made for fulfillment in God, but we are also creatures who seek fulfillment in community with other human beings; we are social, not individual, in makeup. The embodiedness that is ours is included in the drive to find fulfillment in God through various surrogates, and this tells us that sexuality is a means for the deepening of all relationships, with others and with *the* Other to whom in faith we give ourselves, to the end that in the sharing of life together which we know as *human* love we may also share life together in the *divine* Love.

This is the insight (perhaps often unconsciously known) that is behind the common Christian understanding of marriage as in some real sense sacramental. It is sacramental not only because physical contact is employed to express and increase human love but also because the human relationship in love is symbolic of, an expressive medium for, and a representation and effectual sign that enables a deep relationship with God, for God is Love and acts ever lovingly in and toward humanity. We can also see from what has been said above that a Christian must recoil from the abuse or the misuse of sexuality. Such is not only or merely a distortion of human relationships but also, much more seriously, a blasphemous substitution of entirely uncontrolled desire (or "sinful lust," as the prayer book phrases it, although we must remember that lust, as such, can be entirely right, since it means strong or passionate desire, which surely is a valuable element in human experience) for the love which is from God and which *is* God. Human sexuality is a very good thing; its vulgarization can be a horrible thing, since it entails a denial of the mutuality that is toward fulfillment in God.

The sixth Christian assertion tells us that human existence is in defection from its proper potentiality, from the true self, from God, and from other human beings. Despite the popular notion that the church identifies sex with sin, the genuinely Christian view of human nature makes no such statement. Of course the sexual aspect of human life can become (as Augustine saw, and as Freud and others have reiterated in our own time) an area in which proud assertion of self for self alone brings disastrous consequences. But human defection, usually called "sin," is much more than this. There are theological problems here, about which there is no need to speak; certainly the meaning of "sin" must be reinterpreted in accordance with our new knowledge. Talk about inherited sinfulness or original sin can be very misleading, especially when it is interpreted almost exclusively in a biological fashion. The story of the fall, told in Genesis, is to be taken as something true of each of us, not as a historical account of how sin came into the world at a specific time and place in human history. We are indeed inheritors of a past that for millennia has been marked by wrong decisions, followed by wrong acts and words and thoughts; this is our inescapable situation. But we are also in the position of doing our own sinning; that is, each of us chooses wrongly and the consequences of such wrong choosing are tragic for us and for others.

To speak of "sin" is to speak primarily of a violation of relationship with God and other human beings, the breaking of what ought to have been and could be a free mutual give-and-take in love and justice. We are far from the excellence that is intended for us, and we are thus distant because we have elected to be so. In Luther's words, we are "twisted in upon ourselves" (*incurvatus in se*, he says, is the condition of each person); we deprive ourselves of the good which in principle is ours because we prefer cheaper and easier superficial "goods." All along the line we are in defection. To say this does not require us to accept the ultra-Augustinianism of some contemporary Christian thinkers who seem to delight in calling humankind (in a dreadful phrase recently used on British radio by one of these people) "a lot of rubbish." Nonetheless, we must recognize the situation for what it is, especially in these days when non-Christians like Arthur Koestler in England and the late Lionel Trilling in the United States have been so insistent about the facts.

Sin is whatever prevents the human movement toward true fulfillment in God. It is ultimately a *religious* concept, because ultimately it has to do with God and God's intention for us, which is precisely this fulfillment. As Paul Lehmann, the American moral theologian, has told us, "God's purpose for [humankind] is to make them and keep them human," and that signifies a right movement toward God that is also, and by necessity, a right fulfillment of human potentiality. But it needs to be emphasized that the *sins*, in the plural, which we commit are usually not "religious" sins at all, if by this we mean they are conscious violations of God's intention and are committed as being just that. The best way to bring the sinfulness of such sins home to us is to point toward the places where humans in fact act wrongly: in home, school, business, contacts with others, and the like, where by pride, self-seeking, neglect of our neighbors, ugliness of behavior in our homes, and so much else, we often behave in a reprehensible manner *or* we subtly and insidiously treat other persons as mere "things." And yet, with the most realistic acceptance of the sad truth both about us as persons and us in our social situations, we cannot forget that we remain always God's children, grounded in God, being made (if only we are willing) toward God's image, still possessed of an unfulfilled capacity for God.

It is in this context that we may best approach the seventh and eighth points. First, humankind *can* be given a right direction, enabled to move properly toward God, and not only have the capacity to "perceive and know what things" we ought to do but also be given "grace and power faithfully to fulfill the same." I have already discussed atonement, so I need not repeat what was said. In the event of Jesus Christ, where God's Self-Expression or Word was focal and decisive in its human manifestation and action, something has been accomplished. What Prof. Tillich used to call "the new being in Christ" has been realized and made actual and concrete in this human world. Now it is for us to enter into, appropriate, accept, and make real for ourselves that which has been done. I have protested against confining the significance of Jesus Christ to a divine rescue expedition, but the plain testimony of two thousand years of Christianity is that Jesus Christ *does* rescue us in the supreme sense that through his deed, culminating on Calvary, he opens up the right road to fulfillment and provides grace—which, as Kenneth Kirk once said, is God's love in action—to enable us to walk that road, even in times of stress and even though we are quite likely to stumble and fall again and again.

Most of the atonement theologies, as they stand, are incredible and sometimes horribly sub-Christian in their conception of God. But the experienced reality to which they testify—that through Jesus Christ humankind has found deliverance from whatever in their own time and culture they believed to be their worst defect and their most disgraceful condition, however unfortunately they may have phrased the way in which such deliverance is accomplished—is unquestionably a fact with which we must reckon. In my earlier discussion I indicated my own preference regarding a "theory" of atonement (Abelard's stress on God's demonstration of the divine Love-in-act, combined with an ontological grounding of this in the structure and dynamic of the cosmos). But what matters is not this or any other theory but that through a relationship with God, known in act in Christ and in others who have shared the Spirit, God's children may grow in grace, attempting to follow the steps of Jesus' life and coming to be what God purposes for us as "en-Christed" men and women.

But—and here we come to the eighth point—our perfection in this respect is hardly likely to be achieved in this finite world. I believe there is a sense in which John Wesley was correct in speaking of perfection as possible for us. But he was talking about our being caught up into God's love and then put on the path which that love indicates as our true good, rather than indicating some entirely complete state achieved with no further growth required. God has "set eternity in our hearts," says Scripture; there is more for humankind than this world can provide, a richer fulfillment than time and space can offer. Hence there is a certain sort of truth in the otherworldly stress in Christian witness. But there is no place for "*next*-worldliness," which would imply (as Prof. Bethune-Baker once said) putting off to some supposed "next world" what we ought to be doing in this one.

In Chapter 13 I shall discuss such matters—our present existence, shot through as it is even now with "bright beams of everlastingness," in the poet's phrase, and our possible human destiny. Whatever else may be said about that destiny, it is to be seen as *in God*, as humankind is received into the divine life which is sheer Love-in-act. At the end of *The City of God* Augustine used some lovely words: "There we shall rest and see, see and love, love and praise. This is what shall be in the end without end. For what other end do we propose to ourselves than to attain to the kingdom of God of which there is no end?" *How* those words may be understood, what is their *residual truth*, the way in which a process conceptuality can give them a valid significance—all this is to be considered in that later chapter.

12

The Christian Church and the Sacramental Action of the Church

A

In the thought of the New Testament the possibility of there being a Christian who is not also a member of the Christian fellowship is entirely absent. To be a Christian *means* to be a member of the community, for Christianity in the New Testament understanding is by definition a matter of fellowship with others "in Christ." In the first century nobody could be a Christian in isolation from other human beings, although a non-Christian might of course share many of the ideas and engage in something like the practices that marked the Christian community.

It is difficult for us to grasp this fact, especially in the Western world. The increasing emphasis on the welfare state and the socializing of so much of our lives has not yet succeeded in destroying what one of the Presidents of the United States proudly called "rugged individualism." In consequence, the notion that religion is a matter between God and the individual, and that alone, dies hard, if it ever does die. The reason for its persistence is probably that it does contain one element of truth, namely, that religion is indeed concerned with each person's relationship with God, with what that person does with his or her "solitariness," as Whitehead put it when stressing the necessity for each human being to come to terms with God. But at the same time, as Whitehead also noted, the "topic of religion" is the person in society, and that for an obvious reason. It is fallacious to think that each of us is an entirely separate person; as human beings we are members one of another in the solidarity of our race. Enough may have been said about this earlier. Certainly God is concerned with each of us personally, but yet, precisely because we are persons who are necessarily open to and dependent upon others in the commonality of our human experience, that concern is with us as persons-in-society.

Christianity has always been a social religion, even though it has also been a religion which has stressed the enormous worth to God, and therefore to other human beings, of each person in his or her human integrity. Nor can there be any doubt that part of the basic message of Christianity has been insistence on the reality and necessity of what we have come to call "the church." The empirical church that we see around us, and in which Christians generally have their place, is sometimes depressing and often frustrating. But that empirical, visible church, located where we happen to live and which we can see functioning well or ill, is only the hither side—the imperfect expression, if you will—of what the New Testament thinks of as the "Body of Christ" and describes as "without spot or blemish," as "the household of faith," and as "the family of God." To learn to put up with this empirical church is the way both of Christian humility at its best and of Christian growth in God's grace, not to mention the patent fact that such cooperation may do much to make the empirical institution more conformable to its intention and significance as the Body of Christ. As William Temple said, for members of the Christian church it is essential to strive diligently so that (in his words) "the Church will *be* the Church."

The church, in its true meaning, is not simply a human invention or a gathering-together of men and women who happen to share many of the same beliefs and wish to express together their agreement in accepting the same ideals. It is a creation of God. By this I do not wish to suggest, of course, that by some fiat from heaven, or even by some explicit command given by Jesus himself, the Christian church was organized and established. That is not the way in which God speaks and acts in human history. The church's emergence can best be seen as the reflex of the divine Action accomplished in Jesus Christ. It was brought into being out of the older society of the Jewish people ("the old Israel") as the new community ("the new Israel") which was responding in discipleship, in love, in worship, and in service to that which Christians believed God had done in Jesus Christ. It could be described as the corporate response in Holy Spirit to the event of Christ. And into that corporate response those who "join the fellowship" are taken by an appropriate liturgical act—baptism—about which we shall have much to say later in this chapter.

In the event of Jesus Christ, with its preparation in Jewish history, with the occurrence itself as it was received or responded to, and with its consequences in Christian history, God has acted—not by an intrusive measure but by the intensification of the operation of the eternal Word or Self-Expression and with the response made through the Holy Spirit. Out of the situation in which men and women had found Jesus to be their Master and Lord and Savior, God brought into existence the community in which (as John Knox has often said) "Jesus is remembered," and not only remembered as a historical figure but also known through the influence he exerted and continues to exert in a fellowship that looks to him as its head. Thus the Holy Catholic Church is both a society of men and women, hence susceptible to study in a sociological fashion, and also the Body in which Jesus (now taken into God's everlasting life) is still made available to succeeding generations down to our own day. But the church also is not confined to those who are members of it now, for it has included the great company of those who have "kept the faith" and are part of what traditional theology calls "the church expectant" and "the church triumphant."

We tend so to fix our attention on the church of today, called in traditional theology and in the Book of Common Prayer "the church militant here in earth," that we forget "the glorious company of the apostles, the goodly fellowship of the prophets, the noble army of martyrs," and the other holy and humble men and women who have professed the faith of Christ crucified and who have belonged—and still do belong—to the real and essential church much more genuinely and perfectly than any one of us now on pilgrimage in this world. More must be said about this at a later stage.

I have admitted, and all Christians ought readily to admit, the imperfections and blemishes that mar the empirical church in its institutional embodiment; we can see the errors that have marked its history, and we know that not only individual members but the structures of the institution as well are far from being sinless. Honest recognition of this, along with our admission that much pettiness and silliness sadly disfigures the ecclesiastical world, need not rule out loyalty to the mystery of the Body of Christ, although it makes it imperative that such loyalty lead to action that will purify and reform the community as we know it. The sixteenth century heard the cry *ecclesia reformata et semper reformanda* ("the church reformed and always to be reformed"). In our own time the Roman Catholic Church, in its post-Vatican II life, has echoed that same cry. This is why many of us can gladly and gratefully participate in the life of the institution and at the same time feel horror at and express criticism of its imperfections, its errors, and its sin.

In theological textbooks, the church is said to be marked by certain "notes": it is one, holy, catholic, and apostolic. These are useful words, but they have frequently been misunderstood. Rightly speaking, the church is one in that it is united in obedience, worship, and love directed toward God in Jesus Christ. It is holy in that in principle it is different from the world at large, not in order to boast of its glory but in order to be an instrument of God for that world, showing the "fruit of the Spirit" in love, joy, peace, long-suffering, and the rest of the virtues to people who are walking in darkness and doubt. It is catholic in that it is knit together as a social process, with a message that will give life and wholeness to people of every race in every nation and at every time. It is apostolic in that it is based upon the apostolic gospel or good news of God "in Christ . . . reconciling the world to himself" and is truly "sent" (the root meaning of the Greek word behind "apostolic" is "sending"), like its Lord, to bring such reconciliation to the children of God.

Furthermore, the church has certain characteristic ways of expressing its own life in grace, which have developed from inchoate and germinal beginnings and have become the main lines of its continuing historical existence. For example, it affirms in its creeds the faith that is its reason for being. But the creeds themselves are not part of the characteristic structure of the church; they are but ways in which the faith is stated, in language appropriate to the time when they were promulgated, and there is no reason why they may not be revised to state this faith in more understandable terms and with greater factual accuracy—but it is the faith, not the creeds, which is important. The church possesses the Holy Scriptures, which are the record of the formative (and because they come from that earliest age in one sense also can serve as normative) period of the church's history. They provide a proving ground or test for the development of belief, life, and worship from generation to generation, in differing cultures and to meet the needs of different people at different times. Nothing ought to be regarded as legitimate development which is not in line with, although it need not be identical with, that record. Again, baptism and the Lord's Supper or eucharist are celebrated in all the mainline Christian communities; only the Society of Friends and the Salvation Army fail in this respect. Baptism is a rite of initiation for membership in the church and the eucharist is a means of continually nourishing, strengthening, and refreshing those who are seeking to live "in Christ." The church also has a ministry of ordained persons which can trace its historical development back to very early Christian days. It is a ministry adapted to changing situations but still commissioned to serve representatively for the preaching of the gospel, the celebration of the sacraments, the shepherding of the flock of Christ, and the speaking in his name to the world at large. The church possesses, or better is possessed by, the principle of life "in Christ"—a life of discipleship that is not simply obedience to a set of moral truths supposedly taught by Jesus but a life in which "Christ dwells in our hearts by faith" and enables his people to act, insofar as they are able, in conformity with his pattern of human existence.

The New Testament way of summing up these realities of the Christian church's life is in the phrase so often used by Paul, "the Body of Christ." This is not the only description of the church in the New Testament, and it must not be taken in isolation from many others: "Family of God," "Bride of Christ," "new Israel," "household of faith," "temple of God," and so on. But "Body" is singularly apt because it helps us to grasp what is fundamental about the church, perhaps *the* fundamental thing. Let me explain why.

My human body is the way that routing of experiences which constitute what I call my "self" can get itself expressed most obviously in the world and among my neighbors. It is how I get myself across to others. It is through my body that I communicate with them and make myself known to them. Using this analogy, we may say that the deepest meaning of the church is that it is Christ's chief (but not only) visible instrumentality for expressing himself in the world now that he is no longer here in visible ways but is taken into and is part of the ongoing life of God. I have said that it is not his *only* means of self-expression, for if Christ be the one in whom God was signally active, that activity, in Christlike working, still goes on, and goes on wherever there is love, goodness, justice, courage, beauty, truth. But it is, I have said, the *chief* instrumentality since it is the place where he is explicitly acknowledged as Lord, his purpose as sent from God recognized and accepted, even if not always (and this is our human sin) implemented in every respect. Every *member* of the Body—that is, you and I—is to serve as hand or foot or tongue, to push the analogy almost too far, for the expression of Christ bringing God to humankind. This also helps us to see why the church, when it knows its business, is essentially a "missionary society" with a job to do in the world. When the church forgets or neglects its mission, and focuses attention on itself and its domestic housekeeping, it loses its purpose and becomes like salt that has no savor.

In the past half century the several Christian groupings, usually called denominations, have slowly been moving toward restoration of visible unity. There can be no doubt that the day will come when Christians will be visibly one as they are always invisibly united in their faith in God in Christ. In the meantime it is our privilege to serve the particular group to which we happen to belong or to which we feel drawn without ceasing to do all in our power to hasten the time when the several types of Christian emphasis and witness will be brought into a genuine, free, organic unity. Anything that impedes the coming of that unity is a sign of ecclesiastical blindness or churchly arrogance.

We are rightly impatient with the institutionalism of the empirical church when (as is so often the case) it seems to have lost the vision of its purpose. Yet that empirical church can and should welcome into its fellowship those who are seeking life along the Christian way, even when they are impatient. The welcome should not require tests of membership more imposing than those met in infant baptism (about which we shall speak later), where the desire to be a Christian is taken to be present implicitly though not explicitly and where the community welcomes a new member in the confidence that its faith, its worship, and its life are sufficiently strong and sufficiently right to nourish and train the novice. And those who do live the life of the community, seeking to appropriate for themselves its central affirmations, yet unconcerned about the peripheral, secondary, and now and again misleading assertions and practices that have often been associated with those essentials; those who learn gradually to join in its prayers and receive the sacraments, and to read the Bible with open, earnest, yet critical minds; those who endeavor with heart and soul to express in daily life the Christian principle of life "in Christ"—such men and women will find increasingly that they genuinely *belong*. They will discover that slowly they are being made into *Christian* men and women. Or perhaps they will never discover it, being too humble for that—but their friends and neighbors will notice. Dean Inge of St. Paul's in London used to remark that Christianity is "an experiment which becomes an experience." So each one of us, even the least important, can add as he or she speaks of the church and its faith, *experto crede*, "believe one who knows"—one who may not know much, to be sure, but who at any rate has found that life grows continually more meaningful, richer, more integrated in the things that really matter, more adequately adjusted to the divine reality called God, and more sensitive to others who are met each day.

There is a great variety in the membership of the Christian community. One of the ancient Christian writers spoke of the church as a *corpus permixtum*, which my old teacher Henry D.A. Major (onetime principal of Ripon Hall in Oxford) used to translate as a "mixed bag." Another early Christian saying was that the church is a "pool in which lambs may wade and elephants may swim." Both these sayings make the point that the Christian community is for anybody who wishes to be part of its ongoing life, *ongoing* meaning that the Christian fellowship is a social process, as I have already said. The term social process is an adaptation for our purpose here of Prof. Hartshorne's admirable characterization of how things go, and hence how they are, in the world at large; he entitled one of his books *Reality as Social Process*. That manner of putting it helps us to see that like any other routing of events in history and the cosmos there is in the church a past which is remembered and which is causally effectual, a present in which choices are made and action undertaken, and a future which beckons toward genuine fulfillment. There is the inherited past, the contemporary existence, and the sovereign rule (the kingdom of God, in New Testament idiom), which is nothing other than reception into the everlasting divine life, all known in and deeply experienced within the Christian church when it is true to itself.

Thus with all its imperfections and with its great variety of membership, the empirical church reflects and embodies the Body of Christ. Its remarkable capacity for renewal by return to the wellspring of its life is the sign of a vitality which can assure us that even "the gates of hell cannot prevail against it." In the words of an ancient prayer, it is the visible expression of "that wonderful and sacred mystery" which speaks to us and works on us, through the very imperfection, weakness, error, and even the sin of the empirical institution, to manifest in the world of time and space the abiding reality of God's operation in the event of Christ for human wholeness.

I have mentioned the variety of membership in the church —activists and contemplatives, rich and poor, old and young, black and white and yellow, morally concerned and aesthetically sensitive—all are included.

To make my point clear, I venture now to speak very personally. I am a member of an ancient foundation in the University of Cambridge in England. King's College was founded in 1441 by King Henry VI, who laid the cornerstone of its glorious chapel, a building known throughout the world as a splendid example of English Gothic architecture. Wordsworth wrote about it in the sonnet that begins with the words "Tax not the royal saint with vain expense," and John Milton spoke of its "storied windows richly dight, / lit with a dim religious light." Every day, during term, I attend in that chapel the service of sung evensong; on Sundays I am present also at the eucharist that is celebrated in the chapel every day of the week. On great festivals, like Christmas,

Easter, Whitsunday, and the so-called "saints'" or "holy" days, the eucharist is offered with simplicity but with the beauty of vestments and always—as at the daily evensongs —with the singing of great music by a magnificent choir of men and boys. Very likely, I am one of those whose orientation is much more aesthetic than ethical. Certainly I have found over many years that the glory of our chapel, in architecture and music and ceremonial, has brought about a great deepening of whatever Christian faith and life I possess. Nor am I alone in this. Often visitors, and we have hundreds of thousands, say to one or another of us who carry out the chapel's worship, that what they have just experienced is "out of this world." They come from many lands; and they do not mean at all by those words that our worship is unrealistic or unconnected with daily living; they mean, rather, that in participation in that worship they have had a glimpse of something transcendent, more than merely human or natural, something able to give them a lifting of spirit and a deepening of their appreciation of life's significance.

Some might think that this sort of approach and understanding is of little value in the hurly-burly of modern life. I disagree with them. On the contrary, I am sure that it is through just such experience, when Christianity is expressed in just such a way, that many find that "the penny drops, the ice breaks, the light dawns" (to use Ian Ramsey's words for what he styles "disclosure-situations" that give sense to human existence). Through that sort of daily experience, for me certainly and surely for many others, the profound reality of "Christian appurtenance," as Baron von Hügel put it, comes alive. The church as "the mystical Body of Christ, the blessed company of all faithful people," in prayer-book language, with its living members joined with the "great cloud of witnesses" in the past, is vividly known. And all this speaks directly to our human condition.

But what of those who have not heard the name of Christ? What of the non-Christian religions which for millions of people have been their way of making sense of existence and finding value in life? Now that modern travel and highly developed means of communication have made us conscious as never before of those vast numbers of non-Christians, these questions cannot be avoided.

Unfortunately some Christian people (and their theological spokesmen) have taken an intolerably narrow position here. The Jansenist movement among Roman Catholics and certain sectarian strands in the Reformation churches have been prepared to say that such non-Christians are without God and without hope in this world; they have regarded those countless men and women as only what somebody once called "missionary fodder." They have been guilty of the "Christian imperialism" that so troubled the famous historian Arnold Toynbee. But the "great church"—the mainline Christian tradition—has not been so ungenerous. It has been prepared to say, and to find varying kinds of theological support for saying, what their Christian insight should have compelled it to say in any case: that any human being, anywhere, who has shared in love, sought for truth, created or admired beauty, lived bravely, served goodness, stood for justice, and has thus responded, as far as was possible under the circumstances in which he or she lived, to whatever of divine reality has been made known, must somehow be included in the company of the faithful. There has been no doubt that they are numbered among the "saved," even if they have not known about Jesus Christ. Sometimes this conviction has expressed itself in the idea of a confrontation, either in this life or after death, with the person and work of Christ. Sometimes—and this is more in accord with what has been said in this book—it has been urged that *every* access to divine reality (however this may be conceived) which has been opened to men and women is nothing other than the working of the Self-Expressive Activity of God which in Jesus, as we are convinced, is given focal statement in human existence. And to speak in that fashion would be to say, with Dr. Paul Knitter of Xavier University in Cincinnati (one of the brilliant young Roman Catholic process theologians of our time), that we need to "recognize the possibility that other 'saviours' have carried out . . . for other people" the redemptive work which as Christians we know in Jesus Christ. Dr. Knitter adds that "this does not imply simplistically to water down the content of the Christ-event and proclaim that all religious leaders are 'talking about the same thing.' Differences, and therefore unique-ness, are maintained. And thus the universal significance of Jesus is preserved; the difference he makes is felt by Chris-tians to be vitally important for all religions"; but the Chris-tian can also be "open to recognize the 'vitally important difference' of, for instance Buddha"—and he would add other figures as well. ("World Religions and the Finality of Christ," *Horizons* 5, no. 2, 1978: 153.)

Thus the non-Christian religions, and even other world views such as Marxism, may be seen to be genuinely work-ings of God among humanity, since in them enough is granted to provide a sense of significance or value in human life and to learn to live in love, seek justice, do one's duty, and follow truth and goodness and beauty. But if we say this, what happens to the so-called "finality" of Christian-ity? The answer here is partly that Christianity does not claim finality for itself. Rather, it stresses the decisiveness of Jesus Christ as the one who is "important" and (in Professor W.E. Hocking's fine word) "unlosable," because in him there is the "representation," in vivid and compelling fash-ion, of what God is always up to in the world. Finality is probably an unfortunate word to use, but whatever term is chosen, what has just been said is the only kind of finality or decisiveness or speciality that we are called upon to defend. And it is enough.

Is the entire missionary enterprise of the church a mistake, then, if we grant what was asserted in the last paragraphs? The answer here is a resounding No. But we need an under-standing of that enterprise quite different from the one that has often been assumed. The Christian mission is to pro-claim the good news of Jesus Christ, not to denounce other religions. The motive for Christian mission is the desire to share with others what we ourselves have known of God in

Christ. In the experience of Christian people, response to that action of God in Jesus has brought wholeness and new life, and it is unthinkable that it should not be shared with as many others as possible. Certainly nobody is able to say, with the confidence that has sometimes been felt, who will or will not ultimately be saved. God alone could say this, and God is more generous than many who have called themselves by the Christian name. When somebody falls in love, he or she feels impelled to tell others about the loved one; so also if somebody has found wholeness and new life in Christ, he or she will wish to tell others about this—but without damning them into the bargain!

As for Christians themselves, living by faith and in love and hope in this earthly place of their pilgrimage, the unknown writer of the second century who penned the so-called *Letter to Diognetus* gives us the best picture:

> Christians are not distinguished from the rest of mankind either by locality, or by speech, or by customs. For they dwell not in cities of their own, neither do they use a different language, nor practice an extraordinary mode of life. But while they dwell in cities of Greeks and barbarians, as the lot of each is cast, and while they follow the native customs in dress and food and the other arrangements of life, yet the constitution of their citizenship which they set forth is marvellous and confessedly contradicts expectation. They dwell in their own countries, but as sojourners; they bear their share in all things as citizens, and they endure all hardships as strangers. Every foreign-land is their fatherland, and every fatherland is a foreign-land. They find themselves in the flesh, yet they do not live after the flesh. Their existence is on earth, but their citizenship is in heaven. They obey the established laws, and in their own lives they surpass those laws. In a word, what the soul is to the body, this the Christians are in the world. The soul . . . dwells in a mortal tabernacle; so Christians sojourn among perishable things, while they look for the imperishability which is in the heavens.

B

The church of Christ is the fellowship of Christian believers, the "family and household of faith." It is Christ's body, his continuing instrument whose only reason for existence is the doing of his work and the making available of wholeness of life in him. This community is entered by the sacrament of baptism; its members are nourished in their Christian discipleship through the sacrament of the Lord's Supper, the holy eucharist, the mass, the Holy Communion.

What is a sacrament? The catechism of the older Book of Common Prayer defines it as "an outward and visible sign of an inward and spiritual grace given unto us, ordained by Christ himself, as a means whereby we receive the same and a pledge to assure us thereof." In a sacrament, a material and visible—in brief, a "sensible"—thing or action is taken and used by God, in accordance with the will of Christ (whether that is by direct institution, as with the eucharist, or through what Christians believe to be by the Spirit in the life of the fellowship, as with baptism), to convey and to effect a spiritual, invisible result. In the most profound sense, Jesus Christ himself is the supreme sacrament because in him a human life in its complete integrity was taken and used by God as an instrument for the accomplishment of God's purposes. So also the life of each of us is sacramental, for our physical bodies are our instruments for the expression of our purposes, our goals, our aims, and indeed our very selves. The created world as a whole has the same sacramental quality, we may add, since in it the unseen and spiritual is mediated in and through the material. In the final reckoning, God is self-expressed through the whole creation in just such a sacramental or "incarnational" manner, making that creation "God's body." Hence, as process thought has understood, God and the world are indissolubly related.

Thus sacramentalism in the right sense is both natural to human beings and natural to the world, and it is also the way in which God effectively works in the creation. It is entirely appropriate, therefore, that both the Christian rite of initiation into the community of faith and the chief Christian action of worship should have this sacramental nature. Here we shall speak about those two sacraments, "sacraments of the gospel," as they have been called. But this does not mean that we need not recognize a sacramental quality in other rites and ceremonies of the Christian tradition—and value them as such. Such include, for much of historical Christianity, what have been known as confirmation, absolution of sin, marriage, ordination to the representative ministry of the church, and anointing of the sick—all these have the sacramental character in which some material agency effects spiritual ends. Hence they are rightly esteemed and used in many parts of the church.

1. *Baptism into Christ.* The Christian fellowship throughout its history has initiated new members by baptism, in which with the use of water and with prayer there is symbolized "the mystical washing away of sin" and entrance is effected into the community in which Christ is known, loved, adored, and followed.

Baptism is not magic. It does not *of itself* produce a result, for that would reduce it to the level of a sub-Christian ceremony which has a mechanical or automatic effect. It is a sacrament, and as such it presupposes faith as well as human cooperation. Its origins are in the baptism practiced by John the Baptizer and accepted by Christ, and in the proselyte baptism that the Jews themselves employed as a means of entrance, by non-Jews, into their religious-national life. In specifically Christian practice it is instinct with the presence and action of Christ who in it accepts as his own, whether they are old or young, those who would be his. Its liturgical expression is a development from the primitive Christian conviction that every believer must share in Christ's death and resurrection, of which baptism is a figure.

An analogy to baptism would be the removal (either literally or figuratively) of a child from the slums of a great city, where the child has been surrounded by influences that might cause him or her to grow up as a young delinquent, into a healthy and wholesome atmosphere where in loving acceptance there will be provided a healthy and glad acceptance, with deep friendships, happy environment, and enriching circumstances. Such a situation is the Christian fellowship, which even at its apparently least promising represents (however imperfectly) something of the goodness and grace of its Lord. To belong to that fellowship is to be put on the path to fullness and wholeness of life. Thus to be made "a very member incorporate in the mystical Body of Christ" is to have the root of the matter in one. But as we have said, this is not magic. That is why there are parents or other sponsors in baptism. It is also why the Christian initiate must do his or her part to see that the possibilities there offered may through response of the recipient of baptism be brought to fruition.

But there may be more. We cannot tell in what mysterious ways, hidden from us but nonetheless effectual, the act of baptism can produce a difference in personal response to the responsibilities and privileges of life in the world. Nowadays we are so well informed about our "subconscious" experience that we may very well think such influences can be at work. In any event, we have no right to refuse this opportunity to any who, either by their own adult act of commitment or through the earnest decision of their parents, can be brought within the ambit of the Christian community where God's care, as made available through Christ's deed in the world, may have its effect. This is both the rationale for and the justification of the age-long practice of baptizing infants.

Much that has been said traditionally about "washing away sin" is hardly applicable to infant baptism, to be sure. But the main stress in the sacrament is found not so much in that kind of talk (which may be appropriate enough for an adult) but in the simple words with which the minister of baptism signs the baptized person with the sign of the cross as he or she is "received into the congregation of Christ's flock": that "hereafter he [or she] shall not be ashamed to confess the faith of Christ crucified, and manfully to fight under his banner, against sin, the world, and the devil, and to continue Christ's faithful soldier and servant unto his [her] life's end." There is indeed in baptism the assurance of forgiveness of sins to those who repent; but above all, and chiefly, there is the guarantee of spiritual strength to live as *Christ's* man or woman and the grafting of the new believer into the body of Christ's church, which is "the blessed company of all faithful people."

2. *Eucharist.* Throughout the history of the Christian community there has been one action in which those who call themselves after the name of Christ have found the meaning of their faith most fully expressed. This is the eucharist, by whatever name it may be called in the several parts or groups of the church. It is the specifically Christian way of worship. In it, as an ancient prayer from the age of the church fathers puts it, "the mystery of Christ's dispensation is accomplished so far as in us lies." The same prayer goes on to say that in it "we make the memorial of Christ's death, we see the type of his resurrection, and we are made partakers of his heavenly table." The life we live, wherever it may be, is intended to be a continual preparation for and reflection of that eucharistic feast, "of which" says the prayer as it addresses God, in Christ, "do thou make us ever more worthy, through thy holy, good, and life-giving Spirit."

The eucharist is the visible placarding of the faith of the fellowship whose commitment is to God disclosed in Jesus Christ. Since in him there has been established a relationship of obedience between God and humankind, others are taken to share in that newness of life. The eucharist is the chief way in which this is imparted to them. In itself it is a simple affair: the taking, blessing, and sharing of common bread and wine. But it has been adorned with all manner of beauty in music and action and color. How could it be otherwise, when people for centuries have found so much good in it and when it has come to mean so much to them? This development of ritual and ceremonial around the eucharistic action is a token and manifestation of the heart's devotion. Yet at the same time the stark simplicity of the essential action itself can never be obscured, and when it becomes overladen with detail and hence an occasion for liturgical fussiness, as has happened from time to time, it is blasphemed. The traditional interpretation of the eucharist may be summarized under several heads. First of all, it is an action—something is *done*. The early Christian community did not believe that Jesus had told them to *say* something, *think* something, or *aspire after* something, as his "memorial"; they believed that he had told them to *do* something. They were convinced that he had told them to repeat the actions in which he himself had engaged at the Last Supper, on the night in which he was betrayed. He had taken bread, blessed it, broken it, and distributed it to his companions; he had taken the cup, blessed the wine, and given it to those present. What he did there was rooted in the Jewish custom of meals of table-fellowship. But to the usage at such meals there was now added a new significance: in the table-fellowship of Jesus' people, acting after his example, he would be present with them; his "body" and the "new covenant in his blood" would be there. In some real way, whatever our theory about how it is accomplished, there is a "presentness" of Jesus as the memorial of his life, death, and resurrection is celebrated.

Second, the eucharist has a sacrificial quality. Indeed it may be called *the* Christian sacrifice, for it is the offering of thanks, praise, and prayers, along with bread and wine, to God known through Christ. All that older Jewish and pagan rites of sacrificial worship, sometimes accompanied by what are to us barbaric practices, were seeking to achieve finds its fulfillment in this sacrament. "The blood of goats and bulls" and "the ashes of a heifer" sprinkling the unclean, in words from the book of Hebrews in the New Testament, could not reconcile human existence to God; yet such reconciliation was being sought in those Jewish rites and their pagan parallels. Whatever needed to be done to make men and women at one with God was accomplished through Jesus, supremely through his willingness to die. *Sacrificium est tota vita Christi* ("the sacrifice is the whole life of Christ") wrote a medieval saint—and of that sacrifice of himself Calvary was the crowning moment. The eucharist placards Christ before the world, as we have said. Hence, in the "continual remembrance of the sacrifice of the death of Christ," those who assist and partake are again and again incorporated afresh into the relationship between God and humankind made plain in Christ's own deed. The cross is commemorated not in separation from the rest of Christ's life and work but as the final symbolic expression of a total self-giving to God, in which through prayer and thanksgiving Christians are enabled to share.

Third, the eucharist also cements fellowship between Christians and their Lord through his presentness with them in this sacrifice. As we have hinted, theories about the mode of that presentness reflect an almost presumptuous human attempt to define and describe what can be apprehended only by faith. The reality of that presentness—a word I prefer to the more usual "presence" since it is less likely to suggest a *local* or located presence, which great theologians like Thomas Aquinas and Cardinal Newman have rejected as mistaken—is the fact Christians know. It is associated in an intimate and direct way with the eucharistic elements of bread and wine and their reception, but primarily it is in the action itself that the presentness is discovered to those who attend and receive the sacrament by faith and with thanksgiving. Why need we seek to go beyond this? This is enough. Fortunately more and more thoughtful Christian theologians are prepared to leave it at that and refuse to engage in too much speculation about the *how*.

In the fourth place, the eucharist makes the communicants one with each other, quite as much as one with God. In this "sacrifice of praise and thanksgiving," singing together the Christian songs of joy and kneeling together to receive the gifts, they find not only Christ's presence made real but also that since "he is in us, and we in him" they may themselves "be perfected in one."

In these ways, among others, the eucharist is an expression of the main emphases of Christian faith. It is an action in which Christ is remembered; a participation in his self-offering to God, with thanksgiving and praise as the human response; a feeding of the believer with the life of God made available in Christ; fellowship with God and with neighbors, and, as a consequence of all these things, the imperative and the power to live a life of love in the world. In the last words of the old Latin mass, *Ite, missa est*. The action is done; go out now into the world to love and serve the Lord in the men and women who are our neighbors, friends, and acquaintances, wherever we live and work.

Associated with this sacrament are the other rites and ceremonies, the public worship and occasional services, of the church. The daily offices of morning and evening prayer, the litany, the penitential offices, the provisions made for the care of the sick, the marriage of Christian people, the burial of the dead—these are all part of the great traditional experience of public or "common" prayer and praise, and they further establish us in relationship with God in Christ. For each of us personally there is also the practice of so-called private prayer, in which through daily devotion life in Christ is nourished and strengthened. I shall not speak here about this, my own views on the matter may be found in a little book written some years ago, *Praying Today* (Eerdmans, 1974), in which an effort was made to meet some of the problems and answer some of the questions that personal devotion may suggest.

Finally, one other Christian practice should be noted. This is the possibility of personal and private confession of sin, in the presence of an ordained minister of Christ's church, as a way in which the forgiving and healing charity of God is brought home to those who are troubled in conscience and need reassurance and assistance. For many years the several churches of the Reformation tended to look with suspicion on this practice; more recently, some of them have recognized its value and have urged their ordained clergy to commend it to their people in whatever form may seem suitable. To many who are deeply troubled, public statements of absolution are not quite adequate. In a person-to-person relationship such as the private confession of sins there is possible a strengthening and refreshing of confidence in the loving-kindness of God shown toward humankind. It should not be forgotten in this connection that the ordained minister is not the one who forgives the sin. God alone can do that. But the minister can declare and pronounce to God's people *God's* absolution and forgiveness of their sins.

It remains only to say that alteration of the wording of much of Christian worship, with the eradication of sub-Christian ideas that have been allowed over the centuries to creep in and still remain to deform worship, and with the necessary implementation of the traditional rites by new vistas of divine truth that have been vouchsafed to later ages, not least our own, is an urgent task for today's Christian fellowship. No one of us can know and see the depths of God's self-revelation. It is by common participation in the common life of a great tradition that each of us can find a deepening and enriching of faith. We do not need to be uncritical, but we must be humble. The task of each succeeding generation is to add its own insight, its own distinctive apprehension, to the growing body of corporate experience. Each new generation, as one of my friends liked to say, is "the spearhead of the Christian tradition." Thus it is for each generation to allow that tradition to come alive in its own time and place, to see that it is purified and given contemporary significance, with such modifications as may be required; and then to hand it on to the next age, for the enrichment of the Christian faith, worship, and life of those who follow.

13

Destiny and Resurrection

The beautiful passage from the *Letter to Diognetus,* quoted in the last chapter, spoke of the soul, and had the entire passage been quoted we should have seen that the writer contrasts the soul as imperishable with the body, which is perishable. Although a devout Christian, the writer of that letter had undoubtedly felt the influence of hellenizing thought that was dominant in the civilization of which he was a part; and that kind of thought made just such a distinction between soul and body. Indeed, it could speak of the body as "the prison-house of the soul" and long for the release of the latter from captivity to the former.

This point of view is not compatible with the Jewish way of understanding human existence, and it is in flat contradiction to what we now know about ourselves as human. In the chapter on human nature the position was outlined. We are psychosomatic organisms, not souls who happen to reside temporarily in bodies. We are "wholes," with body, mind, and spirit: And to be a person *is* to be just that kind of organism. At no point is this as significant as when we are considering what may be said, more particularly by Christians who subscribe to the process conceptuality, about our human destiny.

The third word in the title of this chapter is "resurrection." This word is of singular value, since it is an indication of the way in which Judaism regarded human destiny. The Jews did not believe in the immortality of the soul, as did the Greeks; rather, they believed—or after centuries of Jewish history came at last to believe—that the total human organism would in some fashion be raised from the dead and would endure in God. Not that this belief was found in early Jewish thinking, for in earlier centuries, as the Old Testament makes plain, the Jews believed that with death there was an end to human existence. They could speak of the persistence of some strange shadow of that existence in a place called Sheol. But this was a dim and vague affair, presumably taken to be a way in which the "spirit" breathed into human life when God shaped the "dust of the earth," as the legend in Genesis tells the story, would never be utterly destroyed—after all, it had been breathed by *God* and hence must be indestructible even if largely irrelevant to whatever the future, beyond death, held for men and women. After a time, however, some Jews began to speak about resurrection of the body, which to them meant the entire human personality; they did this because it was inconceivable that Jews who suffered death as martyrs in the time of the Maccabees should be "cast as rubbish to the void," their faithfulness to Judaism unrewarded and their bravery denied enduring value.

The Sadducean school of thought in Judaism rejected this development, while the Pharisaic school accepted it and taught it to their adherents. Obviously the beginnings of this belief were somewhat primitive in their understanding of resurrection; doubtless they assumed that the resurrection would be of the person more or less as in the days before death. Later on, Pharisaic ideas were more highly "spiritualized," and Paul, himself a learned Jew before his conversion to Christian faith, probably reflects such notions in the way in which he speaks of resurrection in 1 Corinthians 15. Here he contrasts a material body and what he styles a spiritual one; he rejects the idea that flesh and blood can enter the kingdom of heaven, but he teaches that between the body we now know and the body that is appropriate, in his thinking, to heavenly places there is the sort of continuity he took to be between a seed planted in the earth and the flower or tree which grows from it. This reflects, of course, a mistaken botanical interpretation, although the continuity is there—but not of the sort he wishes to defend.

The important consideration here is that primitive Christianity interpreted the rising again of Jesus Christ in this fashion, and not by a conception of the soul's immortality. Sooner or later, however, that Greek idea made its way into Christian thinking, and today it is doubtless true that a vast majority of Christian people have been led to think that immortality of the soul is the Christian belief, and seek to combine this in some fashion with the talk about resurrection found in the New Testament. It is not a happy marriage of ideas, and it has led to much confusion.

I confess that there was a time when I myself endeavored to reconcile these two and tried to work out a posiiton that would preserve them in such a way that it would still be possible to speak in the traditional fashion of survival beyond death of the human personality. In a moment I shall give the arguments which led me at that time, as they have led many more competent Christian theologians both in the past and today, to talk in a different fashion of survival as a necessary ingredient in the total Christian faith. It should be said now, for reasons which will be given later, that I have become convinced we require what may be called a "demythologizing" of this teaching (following the line of thought of the German theologian and New Testament scholar Rudolf Bultmann). This does not mean outright rejection; it has to do with the attempt to penetrate through the symbolic (and mythological) language which religion inevitably uses to the basic reality that is there being affirmed. One day I hope I can write a book that will engage in just this enterprise; for the moment, I only mention it and in the conclusion of this chapter shall try briefly to say what belief it seems to me to make possible and credible for us in our own time.

But first, what in fact have been the traditional arguments

for life after death, as it has come to be called? Despite my own dissatisfaction with these arguments, it is only right that I should present them as sympathetically as possible. I should also follow them with an account of the traditional view of death, judgment, heaven, and hell, the so-called last things, as they have been interpreted in the historic Christian theologies, although once again I believe that the process of demythologizing is necessary at this point also.

The case that has been put for life after death within the Christian tradition has not been based upon Greek ideas of the supposed indestructibility of the soul, like those found argued in the dialogues of Plato. The real grounds adduced for the belief by Christian thinkers have been the nature of God as disclosed in Jesus Christ and the Christian conviction that this same Jesus Christ has been raised from death. Let us say something about each of these.

In the first place God's love is so real, so intense, that it is thought to be inconceivable that once God has so painstakingly created human life, after such a fashion that the human heart is "restless until it finds its rest in God," God will either destroy that human life or permit it to be destroyed. Furthermore, it is unthinkable that the glimmerings of communion with God, the beginnings of life in relationship with God, can be so ephemeral in their importance that death can altogether finish the bearer of them. The fact of the divine-human relationship, begun in this present life, implies (it is urged) an ever-deepening and ever-widening relationship beyond that which is possible in our human three-score years and ten.

The character of God is thus one of the basic foundations for the Christian hope as this has commonly been presented. And it is based, in itself, on the faith that God is love; if God were not love, then life after this world's fever was over would be utterly undesirable. It would simply be going on and on, in some continuing mode of existence that would have no attraction. The Buddhist desire for annihilation is taken to be proof of this, since with no conception of God, whose companionship could illuminate life beyond death and make it a joy to be desired, such a life would be a fate to be feared and avoided.

The other traditional ground is the resurrection of Jesus Christ. The conviction of the earliest Christian disciples that their Lord and Master had not suffered total annihilation, that death was not the end of him but that he was alive and with them "to the end of the world," carried with it the confidence that because *he* lived, they would live also. Life with Jesus risen from the dead was an experience that began here and now; and since it was *God* who had thus raised Jesus from the dead, Christian believers were sure that life in Christ was indestructible, both for him their Lord and for themselves as those already united with him. This, it was said, is the meaning of the Easter message. "We know that we have passed out of death into life," they asserted, not only because they loved their brothers and sisters (which was a sign of participation in the love of God in Christ) but also because "Christ being raised from the dead will never die again; death no longer has dominion over him." Easter proclaims his victory to the world; and so the earliest Christians could indeed declare that because Christ lives, they also shall live. This is the confident hope that through the gate of death, we will pass to our resurrection.

Notice that *resurrection* is being presented, not simply the immortality of the soul. It is the total personhood—with "all things appertaining to the perfection of [humankind's] nature," as Article IV of the Thirty-nine Articles of Religion in the Anglican prayer book puts it—that has been raised in Christ, and hence it is the total human existence that will be raised for anyone who is "in Christ." This way of talking is a guarantee of the reality and value of that which is done "in the body." In an earlier chapter we stressed the Christian teaching that each of us is a compound and complex organism of material stuff, and of intellectual, emotional, conative, and valuational powers, all of which are necessary for full life in this world. Thus any significant life beyond this world must include some such embodiment—although this does not mean the physics, chemistry, and biology of our present physical bodies, since (in Paul's words) "flesh and blood cannot inherit the kingdom of God." Resurrection is at the very least a symbolic way of guaranteeing that such embodied existence, and also sociality or sharing with others in human existence, count enormously in the ongoing reality of human life.

Thus death has lost its "sting" and the grave its "victory." There is here no "flight of the alone to the Alone," as the Neoplatonic writer Plotinus thought would be the case. On the contrary, there is a social existence beyond death, in which the integrity of human nature will be preserved in both its personal and its communal aspects. Schubert Ogden has said that the immortality of the soul idea has been a way in which personal reality has traditionally been given value idea and the resurrection a way in which social reality has been given value. He is probably correct in this, although the immortality of the soul is, as it were, an alien intruder into the basic biblical picture.

I have said that I am not today satisfied with much if not all that I have just presented. In what follows I shall set down what now seems to me to be the residual significance of this position, once we have engaged in the strenuous and perhaps disturbing enterprise of getting behind the accepted phrasing to the intention which was, as I believe, seeking expression. At the moment, however, I go on to outline the traditional presentation of the four "last things," although once again I shall be obliged to follow them by stating another way in which they may be understood.

The "last things" are death, judgment, heaven, and hell. We *all* die, sooner or later. What is more, *all of us* die, unless we subscribe to the immortality of the soul concept—but in biblical thought that is not taught and therefore the total humanity that each of us is or possesses is believed doomed to extinction. Resurrection after death is the raising or reconstitution of total humanity; it does not presuppose some element in human existence which naturally persists after the death of the body. We have already indicated that no Jew would have been able to talk about "John Brown's body amoldering in the grave, while his soul goes marching on." Body and soul, John Brown would die; so early Christian thinking said, in agreement with Jewish thought.

But we are judged, and this judgment is stated in Christian tradition as being every day of our lives as well as at the point of death. The latter is usually styled "the particular judgment" in that each person is evaluated or appraised, at the end of his or her mortal life, in terms of the good or the evil he or she has done. That is not the whole story, however, for at the end of the world, when God (so to speak) makes a complete evaluation of the creation, there will be a general judgment. Each human life will then be judged again, in the light of the whole creation's achievement, for good or for ill.

Heaven and hell are the last two terms to be considered here. Heaven is life with God, in the enjoyment of "the beatific vision." It will be the occasion for the rejoining, in some fashion, of soul and body, if the notion of immortality of the soul has been entertained. In any event it will be entrance into perfect rest, although that rest need not be regarded as cessation of all activity by those who are in heaven. On the contrary, as A.E. Taylor once suggested, it may very well be endless growth *in* perfection, once the state of heavenly perfection has been achieved. Hell, on the other hand, is the absence of God. It is that state or condition in which human beings may find themselves if they are judged unworthy, through their sin and in spite of all that God has sought to do for them, of being "with God" for all eternity. Sometimes the picture of hell has been painted in lurid fashion, with ghastly punishment inflicted upon "lost" persons; more frequently, at least in recent theological writing, this aspect has been muted or denied, and stress has been put on such ideas as persistence after death apart from God's presence—or even *in* that presence, which for the utterly unworthy man or woman would be horrifying, as when an evil person is compelled to be with someone whom he or she deeply hates.

So much for the traditional presentation of the four "last

things." Certainly nobody could deny that when they are presented in this fashion they have the capacity to force all of us to regard human existence, human decisions, and human actions as matters of very great importance. They compel those who accept them to live seriously and responsibly; they demand moral integrity and make impossible any cheap, easy, or superficial attitude toward duty and toward obedience to God's supposed commands. To all this I shall return. But before I leave the "last things," it must be added that in many parts of the Christian tradition a fifth "last thing" has been introduced. This is a state beyond death but short of heaven or hell; it is usually called purgatory or the intermediate state. Its point is that at death most human beings are hardly fit for heaven or bound for hell. They may be on their way to the vision of God for all eternity, which is heaven, but they need a period of purification or growth so that they will be in a condition that will make heaven a joyful possibility for them. Here certainly, as in the case of the other four "last things," we are talking in highly symbolic language. That is why modern theologians are unwilling to press such questions as whether or not the intermediate state is temporal or (as some have suggested) quasi-eternal, whatever that may mean.

I now turn to a reconception of human destiny, such as may be suggested in the process conceptuality but which will be as loyal as possible to the general view of things that biblical material provides. Perhaps it will be helpful to some readers. Before I state it, however, I must say that there is no reason why the more traditional position, both about life beyond death as a subjective (and hence personal) reality for each of us and also with respect to the traditional portrayal of the "last things" (including an intermediate state), may not be accepted by those who find it compelling. There is no systematic rejection of this position in process thought. The vision of reality which that conceptuality offers does not make any decisive judgment on the matter, and Whitehead himself said that if there is evidence to support, say, personal immortality for each human life, this evidence can provide a ground for affirming it. Some contemporary process theologians are prepared to accept something like, if not always identical with, that traditional position; John Cobb is one of these. But other process theologians, like Schubert Ogden, would disagree and argue that while there is no systematic reason for rejection there is also no special reason for acceptance. As will be seen, my own view is closer to Ogden's, but like him I am sure that back of, in, and behind the traditional position enormously important assertions are being made, and that these may be stated "in other words" (as a friend of mine puts it) which will yet be compelling and loyal to the intention of the Christian faith. Pastorally speaking, I agree with Robert Mellert, an American Roman Catholic process theologian, who has written wisely in his essay "A Pastoral on Death and Immortality," included in the symposium *Religious Experience and Process Theology* (edited by Cargas and Lee, Paulist Press, 1976):

> The richness of Whitehead's thought is such that it provides a solid philosophical framework for a great diversity of human experience and a means of synthesizing that experience in interesting new ways. It can account for, and indeed deepen, the thinking of traditionalist and liberal alike, and it can also be an effective instrument of translating between their different interpretations of their experience of reality. And this is the fundamental task of ministering to the sorrowing and dying: to understand, support, and to deepen.

To turn now to my suggestions about reconception, I must begin with a refutation of the sharp distinction, often proposed by those who call themselves biblical theologians, between what are said to be the Jewish and the Hellenistic views of history. The latter asserts at best a cyclical return of history upon itself, it is claimed, while for the former there is a goal, "a good time coming," in which the purpose of creation will be accomplished. In the cyclical view the historical process can have no significance, and human beings may properly seek to extricate themselves from it; in the Jewish view history is getting somewhere and the happiness of humankind is in their aligning themselves with the purpose that runs through it and hence sharing in the accomplishment of that purpose in the "end." This very sharp distinction is in fact not the case, but there *is* a sense in which it may rightly be asserted that the Bible speaks of God's working through history toward a goal, whereas the Greek position failed to stress this, even when it was theistic in outlook. The biblical position is that God is *in* the creation, though not exhausted by it. Therefore time, succession, and a dynamic conception of historical events are affirmed by biblical writers. History, then, makes its contribution to God, although *how* this can be the case is not always clear.

Another error of "biblical theologians" is that of making too sharp a distinction between history and nature. These theologians sometimes talk as if the Christian need have no concern for nature, save as a kind of background for the really significant thing—which is the historical movement of humankind and of nations. Such a dichotomy is untrue to the scriptural witness, just as would be the opposite idea that dissolves history into nature. The fact is that the Bible makes us read nature in terms of history. It is indeed the background, the setting or context, for human experience and history, but it is also in itself a historical process that the Bible portrays as moving from inchoate beginnings (when, as the myth in Genesis puts it, "the Spirit of God was moving over the face of the waters") to the consummation of all things (when, as Revelation says, there shall be "a new heaven and a new earth"). The real distinction between some philosophical ideas, which are nonbiblical in their implications, and the scriptural picture is exactly what I urged above: that between history read in terms of nature and nature read in terms of history. Interestingly enough, recent study of the physico-chemical world seems to be producing results that are on the side of the scriptural reading of the matter.

But, it may be asked, what has this discussion of views of history and of the relation of history and nature got to do with the subject of the present chapter? I should reply that it has a great deal to do with that subject. Briefly, the point is that talk of human destiny must find its proper context in talk of the cosmos at large. In other words, what is God doing in the whole creation, not just in human existence? And we have already emphasized again and again that what God is "up to" in the creation, as well as in human life, is the bringing to actual realization of the potentialities which are given to both in the very fact of their being created. The whole world is the field of divine operation; so is human experience and human history. In the constellation of preparation, person, act, apprehension, and response in community—which was seen in the coming of Christ and what that coming brought about—we have a microscopic picture of what macroscopically is the truth about the world, both in the realm of history and in the realm of nature. And God who is Creator, and who as Creator is "with the creation" (in Whitehead's words), is also God who is the Consummator, in whom the creation's accomplishments are received, treasured, and used.

The biblical myths have something to tell us here. The myth of creation is not literally or scientifically accurate, but it is an invaluable symbolic way of stating that without the divine energizing nothing at all would happen in nature or in history. The myth of the divine consummation (found in books like Revelation in the New Testament and suggested by the picture of resurrection, as well as by the "last things") is an assertion that the divine purpose cannot fail, that God will take into the divine self what is achieved in the world, and that in some fashion, obviously beyond our imagining, God will be disclosed as all in all. As God's love is the ultimate dependability and the chief creative cause of all things, so also God's love is the final end and the fulfillment of all things. It is in no sense a contradiction of this biblical view if we feel obliged to say, as process thought would suggest, that creation is an everlasting activity. In that case God still remains what I have styled the "ultimate dependability" and the "final end." God is still that supreme reality who on the one hand maintains order and provides novelty and on the other hand through the process of nature and history secures ends that are incorporated into the divine self (in the divine "consequent nature," as process thinkers would say), and thus validates and vindicates what is done in the world.

I urge, then, that talk about human destiny through stories of resurrection, like that about the "last things," is a way of saying with the firm conviction of Christian faith in the cosmic divine Lover active in the event we name Jesus Christ that we can put our trust in God for both time and eternity, whatever we might wish to add about our own subjective participation in the divine life. This needs to be spelled out.

In the New Testament, the notion of resurrection finds its focus in Jesus Christ himself. It is *he* who has been raised from the dead; we are then raised in him. Jesus Christ, in the full reality of his existence, has been "taken into God" in a way we cannot explain. This was the initial and basic Christian affirmation about him. For us to be "incorporated into Christ," as Christians believe occurs when they are made his members in his Body (the Christian community, the church), is to share with him in his being "taken into God." And when it comes to the "last things," we can see that death is indeed the finality of our mortal existence, the last page of the book of human life for each of us. But that is not "the end" in the sense of *finis*. Rather it is (or may be) the occasion of our being received by God, as those who are thus participant in Jesus Christ, to be remembered forever just as we are and with just what we have done. So also judgment now makes sense, since we are always being appraised, and at death shall be finally appraised, for what we are and for what we have done. Heaven is nothing other than God, the divine self. God is indeed the kingdom of heaven in God's "consequent nature"; for God cannot have an area or place or sphere completely separate from the world. It is not possibile to talk about God without also talking about the world in which God is acting creatively and redemptively. And hell is rejection, as a surd, from such life in God through Christ. Since it may be the case (we do not know) that some elements or entities in the world have been utterly evil, no place can be found for them in the divine life of love.   Incidentally, much Christian thought and some process thinkers have been unwilling to make any such statement on that last point.   The former would insist that God's love is strong enough—yet never coercive—to win the willing response of every creature in the end; the latter would say that God receives into the divine self *all* that occurs in creation, the good bringing God delight and joy and the evil bringing God tragic suffering—which, however, will be transformed by the deity into an occasion for a further transformation, in turning all evil into possible good.

Some further points need to be made.   One concerns the question of whether—and the way in which—there may be conscious or subjective continuing life for humans when they have thus been "taken into God."   As I indicated earlier, process theologians differ about this matter.   For myself, I agree with what Whitehead remarked in the quotation at the end of this chapter: the question is reduced to a state of irrelevancy when we come to understand that the greater glory of God (which is God's continuing activity in love, not proud assertion of the divine self) is the goal giving its profound significance to what goes on in the world.   Yet some may, and many do, feel otherwise, and I think we do well on this particular subject to accept Mellert's wise words already quoted.

Another question has to do with a practice that those in the "Catholic" churches of Christendom have found so valuable: praying for the departed.   I believe that such a practice can be meaningfully continued, on the basis of the view here presented.   If we are permitted to remember before God those who are now with us, we are surely also permitted likewise to remember those we have loved and lost.   We do not know what effect such prayers will have, but we do know that all generous prayer is valued by God, and while God always does the best that can be done in every circumstance, we may cherish the thought that God also can use prayer of that kind for furthering the divine purposes for good, though it may be in a way past human comprehension. It should not be forgotten that we do not know in what fashion *any* prayer made at any time is effectual, yet we *do* feel ourselves impelled to pray for ourselves and our friends as much as to pray for all good causes and actions. We know that commiting oneself to God, letting oneself be lifted into God's presence, is one of the ways we become truly human. And we have every reason to believe that in this lifting of self to God we may include all persons and causes that we hold dear or consider worthy, trusting that in God's own way and in accordance with the divine loving intention God will use such remembrance for the good of the whole creation. And if nothing else could be said, it would still be possible to affirm (from our own experience) that the love we have felt for the departed is confirmed and strengthened by such praying, whatever may be its final use in the eyes of God.

The last matter to be considered has to do with what might be styled "Christian optimism." A Christian should not be sentimental about the world; he or she must be realistic. Yet the Christian affirms that God is distilling love, goodness, truth, beauty, and righteousness out of the changes and chances of nature and human existence. *God* can never be finally defeated, although our own small causes and purposes may well suffer such defeat. The only ground for Christian hope is in *God,* but such hope enables us to live with high courage, despite all that may be wrong or evil in our experience, and in ourselves.

A few days before his death in 1947, my philosophical master Alfred North Whitehead, the founder of process thought, had a conversation with his friend Lucien Price. Price kept a record of his many conversations with Whitehead, from their first meeting in April 1934 until just before Whitehead's death, in his eighty-seventh year, on December 30, 1947. The conversations were later published under the title *Dialogues of Alfred North Whitehead.* I quote from the Mentor edition of 1956 what are Whitehead's last recorded words:

God is *in* the world, or nowhere, creating continually in us and around us. This creative principle is everywhere, in animate and so-called inanimate matter, in the ether, water, earth, human hearts. But this creation is a continuing process, and "the process is itself the actuality," since no sooner do you arrive than you start on a fresh journey. In so far as man partakes of this creative process does he partake of the divine, of God, and that participation is his immortality, reducing the question of whether his individuality survives death of the body to the estate of an irrelevancy. His true destiny as co-creater of the universe is his dignity and his grandeur [p. 297].

These words say admirably what a process conceptuality would tell us. When to them is added the Christian conviction that God is the divine creative Love, personalized and personalizing, who was decisively active in the pure unbounded love which was Jesus in his total human deed; and when there is added also the corollary of that conviction, the certainty that God, so understood, receives into the divine unending life the good that has been accomplished in the created world by the free decisions of humankind—when we add these we have a portrayal of human destiny and a way of understanding the true significance of resurrection. For me, and I believe for many others too, this is enough to give our human existence a value and importance which nothing can shake or destroy.

14

Conclusion

This book has been an attempt to present and explain a way of looking at ourselves, our world, and God which is characterized by an emphasis on "process." We have distinguished, of course, between such process and the idiotic and superficial notion of inevitable progress. Our concern has been to emphasize the way in which the world, ourselves in that world, and the supremely worshipful reality we name God are all best understood in terms of movement, becoming, belonging, and significant decision. And we have sought to show that in many fields of human experience this perspective provides helpful and important insight into what is going on in every range of experience.

It has not been possible to discuss each and every aspect of our life in the world. Some areas of that experience have been selected in the hope that these may be illuminated by the adoption of this process conceptuality. Many other areas have not been mentioned, since I have neither the ability nor the knowledge to discuss them. In my book *The Vision and the Way* (the Stephen Keeler Lectures at the University of Minnesota, published by Forward Movement Publications in 1973), I made some comments on such matters as social responsibility, race relations, family life, and so on, but these were necessarily tentative and at best only suggestive. Nonetheless, I am convinced that acceptance of the process conceptuality—whether in highly intellectual terms or in simpler ways—will help us greatly in our effort to live humanly in the world as we now know it to be.

In this book my stress has been on such areas as education, the arts, humanities, science, morality, and above all on religious issues. The second part of the book has focused attention on the way in which Christian faith may be illuminated and its basic affirmations made intelligible through just this conceptuality. That is the best I can do. It is for others, better informed and more instructed than I, to continue this enterprise and show more adequately the ways in which process thought enables us to see "things entire" and in a new light and thus enables us to live more richly and meaningfully.

As we come to the end of our discussion, I wish to return for a moment to the specifically Christian concerns which seem to me, as one who wishes to be integrally Christian in every aspect of my existence, of great importance to those of us who inherit the Christian tradition and, sometimes almost in spite of ourselves, live within the Christian culture.

I am convinced that what we need today is a radical reconception of the Christian tradition in which we stand and from which we look at things. This means that we are desperately in need of a new approach to and a new statement of the abiding Christian conviction that God is made known to us through the "Galilean vision," or what has been styled in this book "the event of Jesus Christ." In earlier chapters I have made some suggestions about such a reconception, and here I shall not develop the matter in any more detail. But in Christian worship the same necessity is present. Our inherited services of worship—our prayers, our hymns, and many of the other things that are part of that worship—are not only less than fully Christian in statement but also impossible for us to accept if we have any regard for intellectual integrity, for honesty, and for relevance to the concrete situation in which we find ourselves. Furthermore, our understanding of Christian moral principles and their application again requires just such a thorough revision. No longer can we live as if we were in an earlier age, when ethical teaching was either ignorant of what we now know to be the case or unwilling to give due recognition to human existence as we have come to understand it.

In other books, those of us who are process thinkers have endeavored to work out a theological or religious position, an interpretation of Christian prayer and worship, and a moral attitude, which will take account of what we have learned but which will also be in genuine continuity with the past we have inherited. Here I can only say that without some such awareness of novelty, coupled with a profound loyalty to the deepest intention of our inheritance, we shall be either last-ditch defenders of impossible positions and ideas or victims of the cult of the merely contemporary. How we should now proceed must be worked out with devotion and with intelligence. It is for others to make suggestions and to experiment in these areas.

So I conclude this book with a plea that our new situation, with its challenge to adventure, with its openness to change, and yet with its inescapable relationship to our inheritance from the past, requires us to think again, to work through once more, the things that are both human and Christian. I am not pessimistic about the future, not only because I have come to feel great confidence in the integrity of the younger generation now coming to maturity but also because I am convinced that in the whole enterprise the divine reality we call God, which is nothing other than supreme, enduring, indefatigable, indefeasible, and unfailing Love, is calling us to be (in Whitehead's words) "co-creators" who respond, however faltering and defective may be that response, to the divine imperative. In any event, in the receptive nature of God our efforts will find their acceptance, and we may hope that they will be genuine and enriching contributions to God rather than disappointing and negative contributions. In God is our basic trust and confidence, not in ourselves and our feeble efforts. Thus we may be both encouraged to do our utmost and comforted in our failures. So the next-to-last word is this: Thanks be to God who is the unfailing dependability in all things.

Yet piety for the saintly founder of my college in Cambridge, King Henry VI, leads me to let him have the very last word. King Henry wrote a prayer that he was in the habit of repeating in his devotions; and we repeat it often in our services of worship in his glorious chapel in the college he founded. The prayer is addressed to the "Lord Jesus Christ," and in being thus addressed it reflects the theology (to which King Henry of course would have subscribed) that regards the Jesus of history and the eternal Word of God as so much identical, so much one, that prayer may properly be spoken to Jesus. One could wish that King Henry had followed the line taken by Thomas Aquinas and prayed (as Aquinas says is correct) *to* God the Father, *through the mediation of* God as eternal Word, and *in* the Holy Spirit—this, in Aquinas' view, was the norm for all Christian prayer, devotion, and worship. As we ourselves have urged in discussing the significance of Jesus Christ, for Christian faith the eternal Word or God's Self-Expression worldward is focally and decisively active in the man Jesus—in traditional idiom, the Word is incarnate in his manhood.

But this theological qualification of Henry's prayer does not make the prayer itself any less moving or any less appropriate as the last word in this book. Here it is: "O Lord Jesus Christ, who hast created and redeemed me; thou hast brought me to where now I am. Thou knowest what thou wouldst make of me; do with me as thou wilt, for thy loving mercy's sake. Amen."